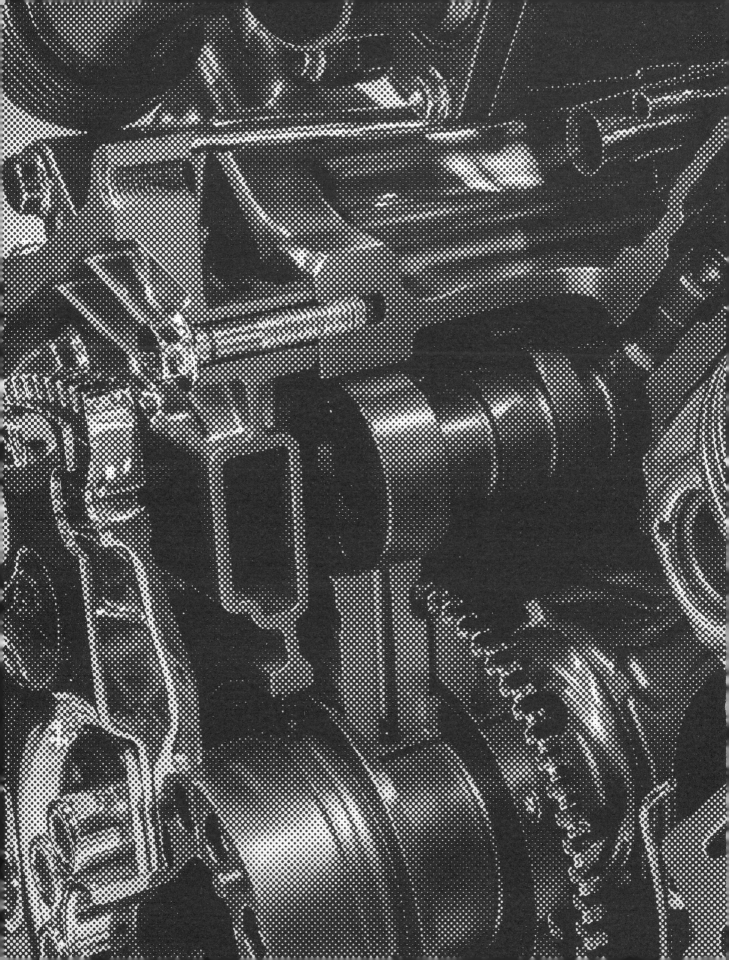

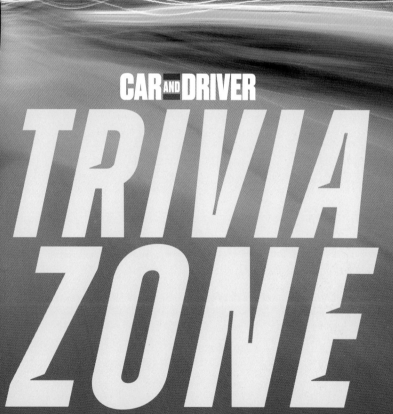

CAR AND DRIVER

TRIVIA ZONE

DAN BOVA

kids
HEARST
HOME

CONTENTS

HOW TO USE THIS BOOK

?

Hey car kids! We've printed the trivia answers a page or two after each question. So after you make your guesses, turn to see if you got them right (no peeking!). Often, there are multiple answers on a page, so stay in your lane and just focus on the answer you're looking for! There are six chapters of this book, with each devoted to a specific car topic. Feel free to read through in order or flip around— the only rule of this book is to enjoy yourself (well, also, no peeking at those answers!).

HERE WE GO!

Ready to take the most fun driver's test ever?

The editors of *Car and Driver* magazine love nothing more than fast, cool cars. (Okay, maybe we love cookies *a little* more.) We know you love radical rides and mean machines just as much, so we put together this trivia book just for you. It's packed with amazing facts about everything from tracks to engines, racers to rallies, and more—plus it's filled with awesome photos of the most incredible vehicles on the planet!

From supercars and NASCAR to a two-headed truck (see page 105), we've got everything a car-obsessed kid like you wants (except maybe a free Lamborghini). So shift your mind into high gear:

Just like racetracks themselves, some of these questions are going to be easier than others. But whether they're no-brainers or head-scratchers, we promise that they're all fun!

All right, ready to learn and laugh along the way? Then sharpen your pencil and your brain, because off we go!

CHAPTER ONE

UNDER THE HOOD

Check your knowledge

of how cars work.

Genesis GV-60

QUESTION 1

Electric vehicles (EVs) are powered by electricity (well, duh). Besides the gas tank, what is another common car part you won't find on an EV?

A. Windshield wipers   B. Tailpipe   C. Seats

Turn the page for the answer. >

ANSWER 1

B. Tailpipe

Tailpipes are part of the exhaust system of fuel-powered cars that expel waste gases from the engine. Guess what? EVs don't use fuel, so there's no gas to force out. (Well, maybe there is if the car had beans for lunch.)

QUESTION 2

Can you match the name of the part to the picture?

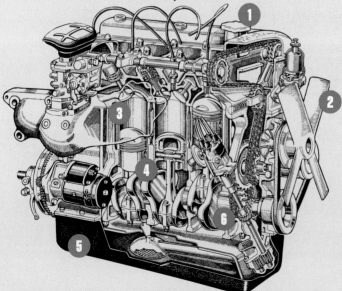

A. Cylinder   C. Engine block   E. Oil cap

B. Piston   D. Crankshaft   F. Fan

WHAT MOVES YOU?

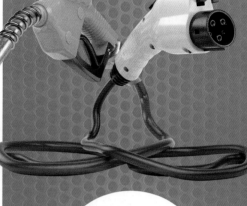

An electric car is powered by:

A. an engine

B. a motor

A gas or diesel car is powered by:

A. an engine

B. a motor

Turn the page for the answer. >

QUESTION 4

Match the car to the animal it is named after.

Cobra   Impala

Mustang   Jaguar

QUESTION 5

Ferrari filed a patent for a system for its future all-electric supercars. What will it do?

A. It turns cars invisible.

B. It cures carsickness.

C. It makes fake engine noises.

QUESTION 6

MOTOR MATH If you subtract the number of doors on a coupe from the number of doors on a sedan, how many doors do you have left?

A. Two
B. Four
C. Zero—pull over, this isn't safe!

1E, 2F, 3A, 4B, 5C, 6D

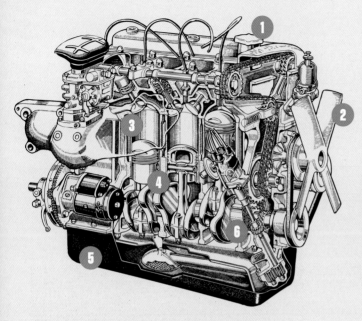

3A: Cylinder: Inside each of an engine's cylinders, fuel burns and moves a piston, which generates power.

4B: Piston: A piece of metal that fits perfectly within the cylinder and moves up and down, turning combustion energy into the kind of energy that spins tires.

5C: Engine Block: A large case that contains most of the internal parts of the engine.

6D: Crankshaft: A shaft that runs the length of the engine block that is rotated by the up-and-down force of the pistons and turns the tires.

1E: Oil Cap: Makes sure oil stays in the engine's oil pan. Oil is needed in an engine to keep all of the moving parts lubricated and moving smoothly.

2F: Fan: Spinning blades that blow air, just like a box fan or ceiling fan, to help keep the engine cool. If an engine gets too hot, it can be severely damaged or even catch fire!

ELECTRIC CARS HAVE MOTORS, AND GAS- OR DIESEL-POWERED CARS HAVE ENGINES.

While the words engine and motor are used pretty interchangeably, most carmakers categorize them this way. An engine is powered by fuel and a motor by electricity. Here's an easy way to remember:

enGines use Gas
moTors use elecTricity

Come on, car companies, can't you name a car after something cute and cuddly like a chipmunk?

IMPALA

JAGUAR

MUSTANG

COBRA

C. It makes fake engine noises.

Electric motors are whisper quiet, so Ferrari will add tech to its future EVs that will make their signature revving noises even in cars without internal-combustion engines. The sounds change depending on how hard you step on the accelerator pedal. Guess that's cooler than you screaming "Vrooom!"

Wow!

The SF90 Stradale is Ferrari's first hybrid. Its internal combustion engine works with three electric motors to make it go—fast!

A. TWO! A sedan has four doors; a coupe has two. We'll let you do the math!

QUESTION 7

Car designers sometimes like to use fancy terms for simple things. Can you point to the "DLOs" on this car?

A. Side windows   **B.** Exhaust pipe   **C.** Squashed bug on windshield

QUESTION 8

WHAT IS A SUSPENSION?

A. When your car gets in trouble and isn't allowed to go to school for a week
B. The system that absorbs bumps in the road
C. The tiny particles that float around in gasoline

YUCK ALERT!

Which has
more germs?

A.
Toilet seat

B.
Steering wheel

C.
Birthday cake (after you blow out the candles!)

What's good in the hood?

Can you match the hood ornament to the vehicle it belongs on?

1. Spirit of Ecstasy　　2. Ram　　3. Bulldog　　4. Dancing Elephant

A. Ram

C. Bugatti

B. Mack Truck

D. Rolls-Royce

TRUE OR FALSE? A high-tech anti-lock braking system can make a vehicle take longer to stop.

A. Side Windows

DLO stands for Daylight Opening—car designers use this term to describe the area of glass between the front windshield and the rear windshield. Why not just call them, uh, side windows? Because it doesn't sound nearly science-y enough, obviously!

Some Other Baffling Big Words

DRAG COEFFICIENT: How much air resistance a car meets while moving; its aerodynamic sleekness.

TONNEAU COVER: The cloth that protects a pickup truck bed or seats in an open car.

OEM (ORIGINAL EQUIPMENT MANUFACTURER): A company that produces the parts used in a vehicle when it's new.

BELTLINE: The line running around a car's body formed by the bottom edges of its glass panels.

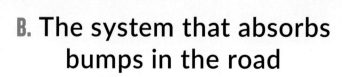

Watch Out!

KING TUT FEARED NO RUTS

Suspension systems have been around for a very long time. In fact, when archaeologists entered King Tut's tomb in Egypt, they discovered several of his chariots buried with him, and the beautifully decorated vehicles actually had ancient forms of suspension systems! Gotta keep the king comfy while traveling over varied terrain, right? And remember, King Tut lived over 3000 years ago!

B. The system that absorbs bumps in the road

There's a system of springs and dampers on the underside of a vehicle that helps keep it protected when traveling over bumpy ground. It also helps prevent passengers from spilling their juice if they hit a big pothole.

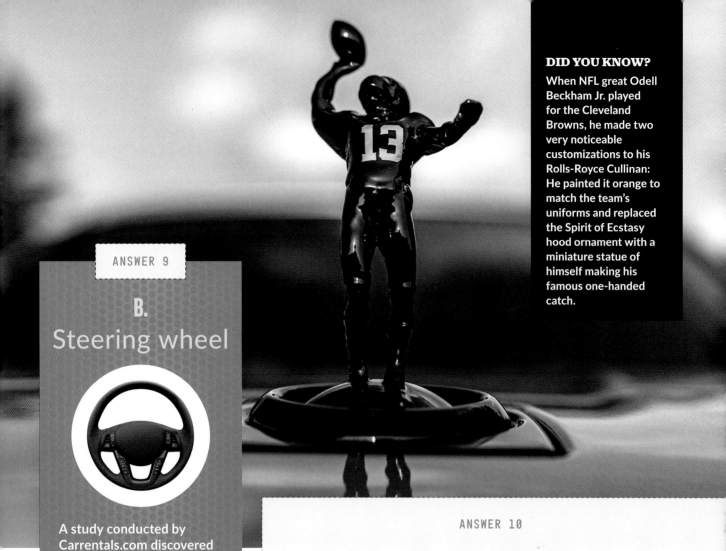

DID YOU KNOW?
When NFL great Odell Beckham Jr. played for the Cleveland Browns, he made two very noticeable customizations to his Rolls-Royce Cullinan: He painted it orange to match the team's uniforms and replaced the Spirit of Ecstasy hood ornament with a miniature statue of himself making his famous one-handed catch.

ANSWER 9

B.
Steering wheel

A study conducted by Carrentals.com discovered that steering wheels are covered with four times the amount of bacteria and germy grossness you will find on a toilet seat. If you were looking for a good excuse to buy fancy driving gloves, there ya go! (By the way, yes, blowing out candles can spread germs on a cake, but not enough to be worried about. Another piece please!)

ANSWER 10

1D, 2A, 3B, 4C

Hood ornaments were originally added to cars to hide the ugly radiator caps that used to stick out in the early 20th century. But as car body designs changed over the years, radiators moved underneath the hood, making hood ornaments more about style than functionality—carmakers kept 'em because, well, they looked pretty darn cool. By the 1960s, though, they became seen as safety hazards in crashes and started getting the ax. Beyond that, you don't see them much these days because designers want their vehicles to be as aerodynamic (able to cut through the air) as possible. Sorry, Ram, no more hood horns for you!

ANSWER 11

TRUE! As weird as it sounds, this safety feature may not shorten stopping distance! By quickly pulsing the brakes on and off, anti-lock brakes keep tires from locking up, which can cause the car to skid.

WHEELS AROUND THE WORLD

Can you match the car to where its company is headquartered?

A. Dodge   E. Volkswagen
B. Land Rover   F. Volvo
C. Maserati   G. Hyundai
D. Mazda   H. Great Wall

United States

Germany

Sweden

South Korea

China

United Kingdom

Japan

Italy

QUESTION 12

Get an earful. See if you can match the annoying noise to the annoying car problem.

1. Screeching under the hood

A. Worn-out brake pads

2. Chugging, choking noise

B. Loose engine belt

3. Squealing from the tires

C. Blocked exhaust

A Jaguar E-Type production line in 1961 in the United Kingdom

Turn the page for the answer. >

QUESTION 14

Before new Jaguars are painted, they are brushed with emu feathers. Why?

A. They are ticklish.

B. Oils in the feathers make the paint extra-shiny.

C. The large feathers can hold an electrostatic charge, which makes them great at collecting any dust on the bare metal.

QUESTION 15

What is a turbocharger in a car?

A. A special plug that charges your phone superfast

B. An engine part that boosts performance

C. The new flavor of Mountain Dew

1B, 2C, 3A

The engine belt needs to have a certain amount of tension to transfer the engine's energy to things like the air conditioning. Too little tension makes the belt loose, in turn producing a terrible sound as it slips.

An engine's exhaust can get clogged with outside junk from the road or soot and carbon buildup from combustion. Like a clogged drain on a sink, it sometimes needs to get cleaned out so that everything starts flowing again.

Brake pads actually squeal on purpose. They are designed with a metal piece that makes an annoying noise as the pads start to get too worn out so that drivers know it's time to get them replaced.

BUT THE WORST SOUND OF ALL?

The one your parents make when the mechanic hands them the repair bill.

A. United States
B. United Kingdom
C. Italy
D. Japan
E. Germany
F. Sweden
G. South Korea
H. China

The top carmaker in terms of revenue (how much money it makes) is Volkswagen AG. In 2021, it made nearly $300 billion. Cha-ching!

EMUS MIGHT NOT BE ABLE TO FLY, BUT THEY ARE NO STRANGERS TO SPEED—THEY CAN RUN UP TO 31 MPH!

C. The large feathers hold an electrostatic charge, which makes them perfect for collecting dust on bare metal.

The big, bendy feathers work so well that BMW and Audi also use them before painting.

SUPERCHARGER TO THE RESCUE!
A supercharger does the same thing as a turbocharger, but instead of using a turbine, it is powered by the engine's crankshaft and provides the engine boost even faster. Someone give that supercharger a cape!

Turbo Speed!

ANSWER 15

B. An engine part that boosts performance

A turbocharger uses exhaust gas to spin turbines that suck air into a compressor and into the engine. The increased airflow allows the engine to burn more fuel, which delivers more power.

QUESTION 16

Many cars have two pedals, but this one has three.

Do you know their names?

A. Gas   **B.** Brake   **C.** Clutch

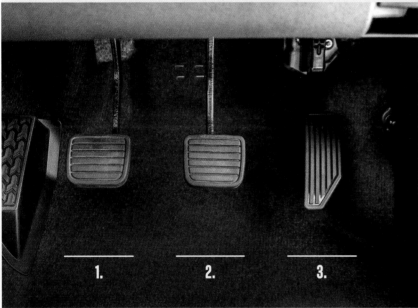

1.   2.   3.

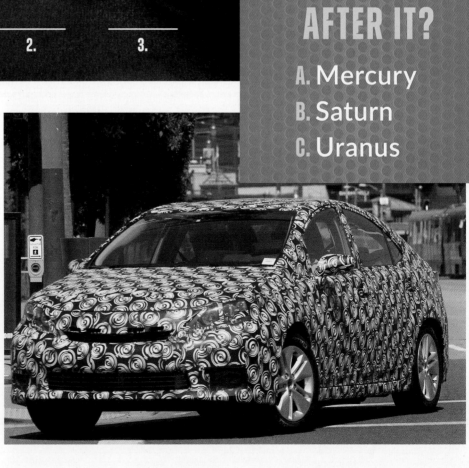

WHICH PLANET HASN'T HAD A CAR NAMED AFTER IT?

A. Mercury

B. Saturn

C. Uranus

QUESTION 17

When companies test out new vehicle designs at the track, they wrap the cars in camouflage to stop nosy photographers from giving away sneak previews.

What do designers call these secret test vehicles?

A. Shy Guys

B. Mules

C. Secret Agents

Turn the page for the answer. >

QUESTION 19

Match the door type to the image:

1. Regular
   ___ ___ ___
2. Scissor
   ___ ___ ___
3. Sliding
   ___ ___ ___
4. Gullwing
   ___ ___ ___

QUESTION 20

What does the "V" in a V-8 engine mean?

A. Very fast

B. Volume of gas it uses

C. The shape the engine cylinders make

QUESTION 21

Which of these is NOT something that can power cars and trucks?

A. Sunlight

B. Old french-fry oil

C. Coffee

QUESTION 22

HOW MANY PARTS IS A CAR MADE OF?
A. 300   B. 3000   C. 30,000   D. 3 MILLION

1C, 2B, 3A

Press the gas to make it go, the brake to make it stop, and the clutch? That's the pedal a driver operating a car with manual transmission needs to press before they can switch gears. (Automatic cars don't need one because they do this, well . . . automatically.)

WHAT IS A TRANSMISSION?

A transmission changes gears in the car's engine to help it smoothly and safely do what you want it to do (for example, go faster on a flat road or work slower and harder to climb a steep incline). Most cars have an automatic transmission (about 98 percent of cars sold in the U.S.), but some drivers prefer the control (and fun) of driving a manual transmission, which involves stepping on the clutch pedal and changing gears with a stick shift.

B. Mules

To help protect their designs from overly curious car enthusiasts (like us!) and competing companies, designers will also put on big pieces of plastic, fake grilles, and other forms of trickery to hide the car or truck's real design.

DO CARS STUDY FOR THEIR TRACK TESTS?

No, cars aren't up all night cramming for their exams, but designers probably are! When they come up with new car models, they build prototypes and put them through all kinds of performance tests to fix any problems before they start making a lot and selling them. Some of those tests take place at closed tracks (meaning no other cars are with them), where they can see how well the cars are able to make quick turns, accelerate, and drive in the rain, snow, and all kinds of conditions. They'll also take them on roads open to the public and use laboratories to get the car working as perfectly as possible. In case you are wondering whether a vehicle's disguise would mess up its performance (like, say, a big fake headlight might make it less aerodynamic), car testers are pretty crafty. They'll only add phony parts to areas of the car that aren't involved in the test. For example, if they are examining the comfort of seats, a bogus spoiler will have no impact on the seat's butt-squishiness factor.

Renault Twingo electric prototype car

C. Uranus

If it makes you feel any better, Uranus, both of those other car brands with out-of-this-world names are now out of production.

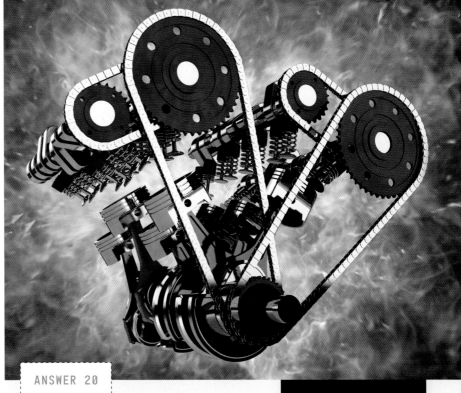

ANSWER 19

1B, 2C, 3D, 4A

Who would have thought there were so many ways to get in and out of a car?

Here are some of the advantages of different door styles:

SCISSOR DOORS

When Lamborghinis were first made, it was hard for drivers to see out of the back window. This style of door allows drivers to open the door and lean out to look while backing up.

GULLWING

Primarily they make the car look amazingly cool, but they also make it easier to get in and out of the car in tight parking spaces.

SLIDING DOOR

These allow rear passengers to easily climb in and hop out. Hurry up, school is starting!

ANSWER 20

C. The shape the engine cylinders make

An internal-combustion engine has sets of cylinders where gas is burned to generate power. The cylinder banks are connected to the engine's crankshaft at an angle, giving them a V shape. So a V-8 means it has eight cylinders.

THE MORE THE MERRIER
In general, the more cylinders an engine has, the more power a car has. This is why, sadly, your family's four-cylinder minivan is never, ever going to beat a V-12 Aston Martin in a race no matter how much Mom floors it.

ANSWER 21

C. Coffee

While caffeine might help your parents stay awake on long drives, it won't keep your car's engine running. But solar power and—yes—even gross french-fry grease have been successfully used to power motors.

ANSWER 22

C. 30,000 From big ol' bumpers to tiny computer chips, modern machines sure have a lot of pieces. (And that's not counting the six-piece box of McNuggets you dropped on the back-seat floor.)

QUESTION 24

Match the number of wheels to the ride:

1

2

3

4

5

6

A. Motorcycle
B. Honda ATV
C. Dodge T-Rex
D. Polaris Slingshot
E. Unicycle
F. Pentacycle

QUESTION 26

There is a rear storage area in vehicles that people from all over the world use to stick in groceries, camping equipment, and anything else they need to haul. Not everyone calls it the same thing.

Match the nickname to the region:

1. Trunk 2. Boot 3. Dickie

A. Europe
B. North America
C. South Asia

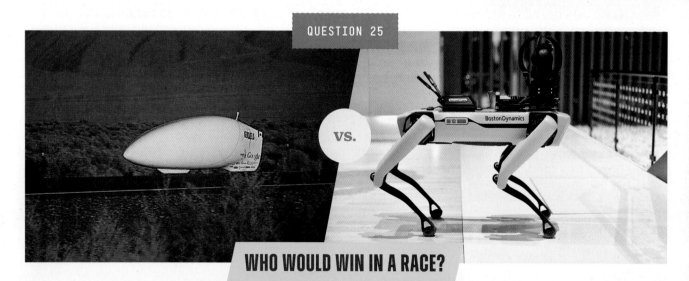

QUESTION 25

VS.

WHO WOULD WIN IN A RACE?

Eta, the Human-Powered Vehicle vs.
Spot, the Robot-Powered Dog

No Hands!

Turn the page for the answer. >

QUESTION 27

A vehicle that can operate with little or no help from humans is called:

A. Self-driving
B. Shelf-driving
C. Shellfish-driving

QUESTION 28

Do you need a license to sit behind the wheel of a car with self-driving capability?

A. Yes
B. No
C. Depends on where you live

QUESTION 29

A car that can drive on land and on water is called:

A. Amphibious
B. Ambidextrous
C. Am sinking

1E, 2A, 3D, 4B, 5F, 6C

Pentacycles were known as Hen and Chickens cycles in the late 1800s. The name describes how the big center wheel (the mama hen) was surrounded by four smaller wheels (the chickens). They were used as postal delivery vehicles, and that center wheel was designed to help carry the weight of the packages. So basically, the Hen was the Hulk.

1B, 2A, 3C

When cars were first made in America, they didn't have a designated storage area, so people would tie trunks to the back bumper. The name stuck!

A. Self-driving

Definitely do not get into a car being driven by seafood! A self-driving car uses high-tech sensors and cameras to capture information about what's happening on the road, and a computer system uses that information to decide if the vehicle needs to slow down, speed up, turn, stop, and more. But don't worry—the computer won't decide to change the music in the middle of your favorite song!

C. Depends on where you live

At the time this book was written, several states had laws requiring a licensed driver to be behind the wheel regardless of the vehicle's level of self-driving ability. But who knows, by the time you read this, robot lawyers may have changed the rules!

Sorry robots, but you're going to have to get speedier if you want to overtake all humans. Boston Dynamics's incredible robot dog, Spot, can do things like walk through dangerous terrain while carrying supplies—but it can't do them very quickly. Its top speed is 3.6 mph, which is nowhere close to the top speeds racers reached at the World Human Powered Speed Challenge. In 2016, the peddled vehicle "Eta" set a record zooming along at 89.59 mph!

Woah!

A. Amphibious

The military uses amphibious vehicles in many operations that start in the ocean and storm the beach. But they're also used for fun, like the Sea Lion, which can drive 125 mph on land and go 60 mph at sea!

HOW DO CARS FLOAT?

Amphibious vehicles have sealed bodies—meaning no water can get in—so they don't sink. (That's pretty important if you want to be even a part-time boat!) The driver is able to switch the engine from powering wheels when driving on land to propellers, jets, or fans when moving through water. The big question we have is if fish use blinkers when making right turns?

Seriously Silly Question

WHAT IS A LEMON?

Just like the yellow fruit, a "lemon" car is extremely sour. Imagine buying a brand-new vehicle, but on the way home, parts start falling off. Your face would be all twisted up, right? Just like if you sucked on a certain sour citrus fruit. That's a lemon—a new car that is plagued with terrible defects and problems. There are lemon laws to help people who plunked down big bucks for a vehicle with big problems ranging from screwy steering to faulty brakes to really bad smells. If the company can't fix it, they have to provide a replacement or give you back your money. That makes us wonder, are there lemon laws to fix smelly sneakers?

CHAPTER TWO

SUPER-CARS AND ROCKIN' RIDES

Test your smarts about the sweetest autos on earth.

Lamborghini
Huracán

QUESTION 1

Why is the common unit of measurement of an engine's power called "horsepower"?

A. In the old days, instead of gas, engines were fueled by horse pee.

B. "Frog power" was already taken by the pogo-stick industry.

C. It is a comparison of how much work an engine can do in relation to a horse.

Turn the page for the answer. >

ANSWER 1

C. It is a comparison of how much work an engine can do in relation to a horse.

In the late 1700s and early 1800s, inventor James Watt was looking for a way to show mill and factory owners how great his new steam engine was. He came up with this unit of measure, horsepower, to show how much work his steam engine could do compared to hooved workers.

Today, horsepower is a little more scientific. It is calculated by multiplying the amount of force (in pounds) by the speed (in feet per second). So if a car's engine generates 200 pounds of force and moves two feet per second, its horsepower would be 400 (200 x 2).

QUESTION 2

The logos of these amazing supercars have been blurred out. Can you recognize which is which from their signature designs?

A. Ferrari   **B.** Bugatti   **C.** Corvette
D. McLaren   **E.** Lamborghini

1

2

3

4

5

QUESTION 3

WHICH GETS MORE INSTAGRAM POSTS?

Put these cars in order of most to least popular on social media.

A. Porsche 911

B. Honda Civic

C. Ford Mustang

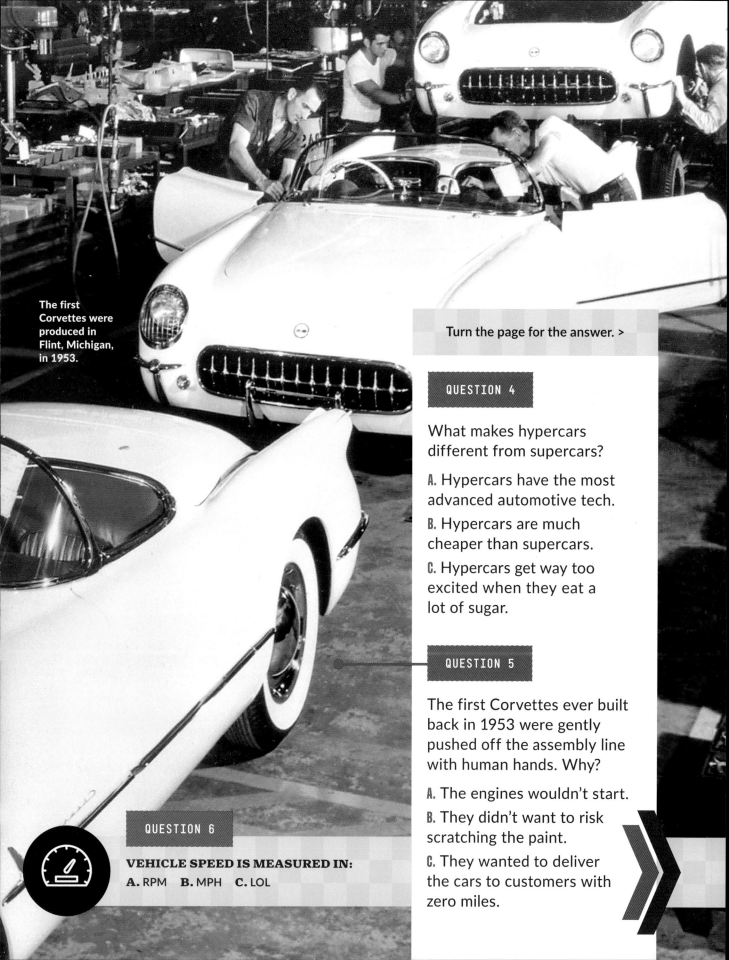

The first Corvettes were produced in Flint, Michigan, in 1953.

Turn the page for the answer. >

QUESTION 4

What makes hypercars different from supercars?

A. Hypercars have the most advanced automotive tech.

B. Hypercars are much cheaper than supercars.

C. Hypercars get way too excited when they eat a lot of sugar.

QUESTION 5

The first Corvettes ever built back in 1953 were gently pushed off the assembly line with human hands. Why?

A. The engines wouldn't start.

B. They didn't want to risk scratching the paint.

C. They wanted to deliver the cars to customers with zero miles.

QUESTION 6

VEHICLE SPEED IS MEASURED IN:
A. RPM   **B.** MPH   **C.** LOL

1A, 2E, 3C, 4B, 5D

FERRARI

LAMBORGHINI

CORVETTE

MCLAREN

BUGATTI

They can't fly, aren't able to turn invisible, and don't fight crime, so what makes a supercar so *super* anyway? There's not a set definition, but in general, supercars have engines with at least 700 horsepower, can cruise at 200-plus mph, and make everyone—even supervillains—stop on the street to snap a pic.

#1 B. Honda Civic

#2 A. Porsche 911

#3 C. Ford Mustang

This might be the only competition that the modest Honda Civic wins against a Porsche and Mustang, so congrats!

A. Hypercars have the most advanced automotive tech.

Think of the NBA. There are plenty of All-Stars, but then you have next-level ballers like Nikola Jokic and Giannis Antetokounmpo. That's kinda like hypercars—they are the best of the best. Hypercars have incredible tech advances, extreme engines that produce monumental power, and . . . well, mega price tags you'd probably need to win the Mega Millions to afford.

Ferrari LaFerrari

ANSWER 5

A. The engines wouldn't start.

Before the Corvette, most modern cars were made with steel. The Corvette was one of the first cars sold with a fiberglass body—a much lighter material—but the new technology caused electrical grounding problems. So, that first exciting turn of the ignition key resulted in a not-so-exciting zero horsepower. But don't worry, the car scientists eventually figured out how to wire things correctly, and the Vette started vrooming!

STICKER SHOCK

In 1953, the first Corvettes sold for $3,498. Compare that to the lowest cost for a 2023 Corvette—just over $65,000!

Today's Corvettes, like this 2023 Corvette Z06, are made with carbon fiber bodies, making them even lighter and faster.

ANSWER 6

B. MPH Miles per hour, meaning how many miles your car travels in an hour. This is the standard unit of measure for speed—unless you live in Europe and have no idea what a "mile" is. Then it is measured in km/h, kilometers per hour.

WHICH OF THESE CARS IS NOT LIKE THE OTHERS?

A. McMurtry Spéirling

B. Chaparral 2J

C. Brabham BT46

D. Pagani Utopia

Can you recognize the supercar by its super butt?

A. Aston Martin Vanquish S   **B.** Porsche 911 GT3
C. McLaren 720S   **D.** Lamborghini Aventador

1

2

3

4

The world's fastest production car (which means it is made in large quantities to be sold to the public) can go a face-melting 330 mph.

Can you spot the speed demon in this lineup?

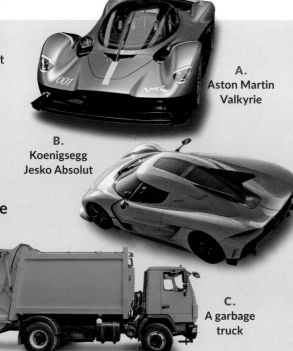

A. Aston Martin Valkyrie

B. Koenigsegg Jesko Absolut

C. A garbage truck

Turn the page for the answer. >

QUESTION 10

The Rimac Nevera, a Croatian-built electric hypercar, had a very, very good day at the test track in May 2023. How many records is it claimed to have broken in a single day?

A. 7   B. 11   C. 23

QUESTION 11

The 1992 Dodge Viper supercar had a Lamborghini-designed engine hiding under its hood. What didn't it have?

A. Built-in side windows
B. A standard roof
C. Exterior door handles
D. All of the above

QUESTION 12

WHICH SUPER SPY IS KNOWN FOR DRIVING ASTON MARTINS?
A. JAMES BOND   **B.** ALEX RIDER   **C.** HARRIET THE SPY

ANSWER 8

B. Koenigsegg Jesko Absolut

The Swedish-made Absolut is an absolute beast, with an engine that can produce 1600 horsepower. Rocketing from zero to 60 mph in 2.6 seconds, this is the car you want if you need to get somewhere in a hurry!

ANSWER 9

D. Pagani Utopia

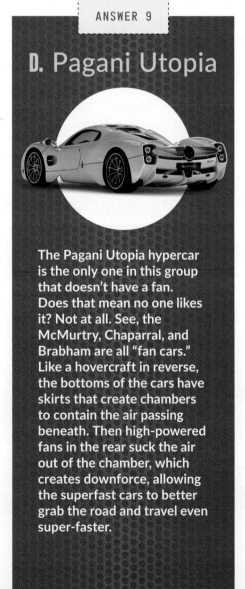

The Pagani Utopia hypercar is the only one in this group that doesn't have a fan. Does that mean no one likes it? Not at all. See, the McMurtry, Chaparral, and Brabham are all "fan cars." Like a hovercraft in reverse, the bottoms of the cars have skirts that create chambers to contain the air passing beneath. Then high-powered fans in the rear suck the air out of the chamber, which creates downforce, allowing the superfast cars to better grab the road and travel even super-faster.

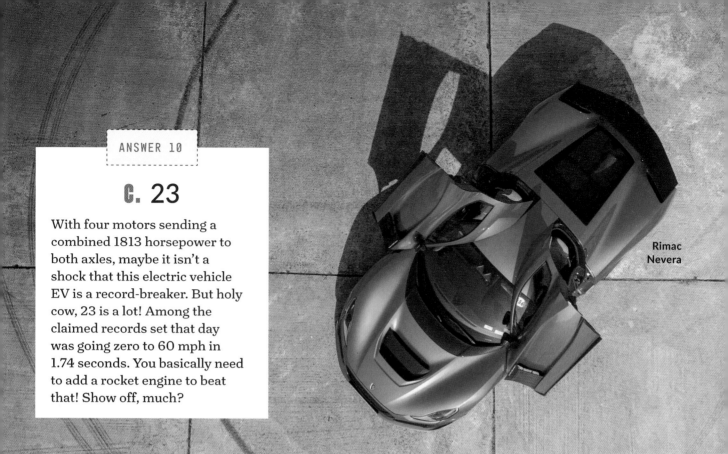

ANSWER 10

C. 23

With four motors sending a combined 1813 horsepower to both axles, maybe it isn't a shock that this electric vehicle EV is a record-breaker. But holy cow, 23 is a lot! Among the claimed records set that day was going zero to 60 mph in 1.74 seconds. You basically need to add a rocket engine to beat that! Show off, much?

Rimac Nevera

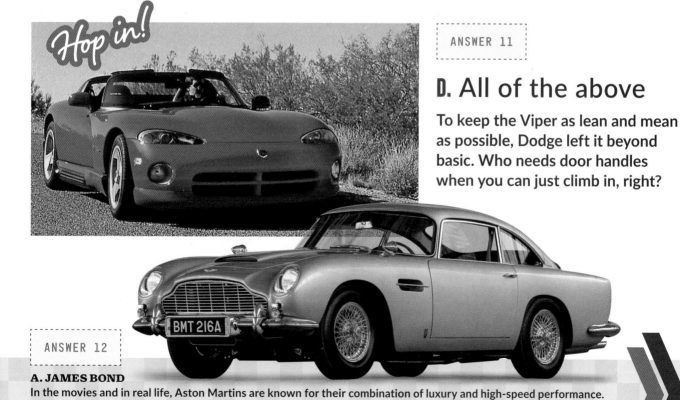

Hop in!

ANSWER 11

D. All of the above

To keep the Viper as lean and mean as possible, Dodge left it beyond basic. Who needs door handles when you can just climb in, right?

BMT 216A

ANSWER 12

A. JAMES BOND
In the movies and in real life, Aston Martins are known for their combination of luxury and high-speed performance. But unlike James Bond's movie version, real-life ones don't have machine guns hidden behind their headlights.

In the 1980s sci-fi comedy *Back to the Future,* Doc and Marty traveled through time in a DeLorean DMC-12. In the original script, they traveled in a much less glamorous household item. What was it?

A. Refrigerator   **B.** Skateboard   **C.** Rocket-powered shopping cart

QUESTION 14

Why wouldn't it be very comfortable to sit in one of these cars for very long?

A. The engines take up all the legroom.

B. The seats are covered in itchy wool.

C. The cars are made entirely of Legos.

QUESTION 15

WHY DOES FERRARI'S LOGO HAVE A HORSE ON IT?

A.
It symbolizes horsepower.

B.
It was the symbol that a famous Italian fighter pilot used.

C.
Ferraris were originally made to collect horse manure on farms.

A.
Flaming Harley-Davidson

B.
Party Wagon

C.
Camaro

D.
Tumbler

Turn the page for the answer. >

QUESTION 16

Match the superhero to their super ride.

1. Ghost Rider

2. Batman

3. Teenage Mutant Ninja Turtles

4. Bumblebee from Transformers

QUESTION 17

Leading police on a high-speed chase is never a good idea for anyone, but why is it a really, *really* bad idea to do it in Dubai?

A. The hot roadways are known to melt the bad guys' car tires.

B. The streets there are really narrow.

C. Police have a Bugatti on the force.

QUESTION 18

Which is the top-selling Porsche model?
A. Boxster   **B.** 911   **C.** Cayenne

THE REAL DELOREAN DISASTER

In 1981, DeLorean produced its first DMC-12. As cool as the DeLorean looked, the company and the cars were plagued with problems—like doors that either wouldn't close or open again—and it all shut down just one year later.

ANSWER 13

A. Refrigerator

It's hard to imagine, but in the first version of this movie's script, the time travelers climbed into a refrigerator that was loaded onto a truck and driven into a nuclear blast. That does not sound nearly as fun as driving a now-iconic sports car!

ANSWER 14

C. The cars are made entirely of Legos.

The design team at Lego Technic used more than one million bricks and took 13,438 hours to build this Bugatti Chiron—totally worth it! On a test track, the Lego Bugatti's engine, which was made up of mini Lego powerplants, got the car up to 12 mph!

ANSWER 15

B. It was the symbol that a famous Italian fighter pilot used.

Italian air force ace Count Francesco Baracca painted a black horse on the side of every plane he flew during WWI. After he died, his mother suggested to Enzo Ferrari that he use the symbol for good luck on his race cars. It was clearly a winning idea!

C. Police have a Bugatti on the force.

The Dubai Police's Bugatti Veyron has a top speed of 253 mph. Good luck trying to outrun that!

1A, 2D, 3B, 4C

Okay, does this count for Bumblebee if his car is himself?

C. CAYENNE Porsche drivers love sleek design, gobs of power, and awesome speed—but they also love a trunk big enough to bring home groceries, which is why the company's Cayenne SUV is by far its bestselling model.

HORSING AROUND

Take a close look at Porsche's logo: Its horse and the Ferrari horse could be twins! Or at least close *ney*-bors.

WHAT DOES A LITER MEASURE IN CARS?

A. The size of the bottle you can fit in the car's cupholder

B. The amount of air and fuel that fits in the engine's cylinders

C. How much windshield wiper fluid it will go through in a year

Where in the world are you?

A. Inside a Storm Trooper's school bus

B. Inside an alien spaceship

C. Inside a 2023 Rolls-Royce Phantom

Which is an attraction at the Ferrari World theme park in Abu Dhabi?

A. The world's fastest rollercoaster

B. The most powerful flushing restroom toilets

C. A Ferrari-only drive-through restaurant

Match the machine to the famous monument from its home country.

1. Lamborghini Diablo   2. Hennessey Venom   3. Citroën GT   4. Rolls-Royce Ghost   5. Nissan GT-R

A. Statue of Liberty

B. Big Ben

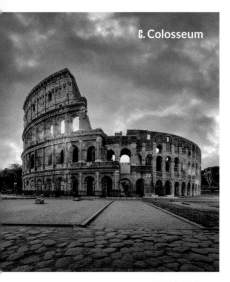

C. Colosseum

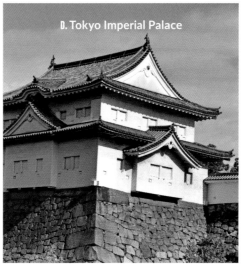

D. Tokyo Imperial Palace

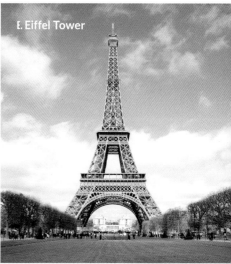

E. Eiffel Tower

QUESTION 23

The most expensive car ever sold went for a piggy-bank-busting $143,000,000. What kind of vintage car was it?

A. Ferrari
B. Mercedes-Benz
C. A minivan made of solid gold

C. Inside a 2023 Rolls-Royce Phantom

Rolls-Royce says that this is the most luxurious car in existence—and looking at it, we pretty much agree. The rear compartment has a privacy panel that goes up or down, super-comfy carpeted floor mats, massaging seats, a refrigerator, an infotainment system, and, yes, its own Wi-Fi. About all it doesn't have is an affordable price. Rolls-Royce Phantoms start at nearly $500,000 and go up (way up!) from there with customizations like sparkling-star lights embedded in the ceiling.

A. The world's fastest rollercoaster

The Formula Rossa is the world's fastest rollercoaster, accelerating from zero to 149 mph in just 4.9 seconds. That's hardly enough time to barf! Compare that to a skydiver, who takes about three times as long to reach a top speed of 120 mph while freefalling to earth.

C. The amount of air and fuel that fits in the engine's cylinders

The kind of car you put gas in has a combustion engine. Its power comes from fuel and air exploding in its cylinders. The more liters the cylinders can hold, the more power the engine produces. The downside of more liters is that the engine burns through fuel pretty quickly. So, for example, a Honda Civic with a turbocharged 1.5-liter engine can go 34 miles on a gallon of gas. A Camaro with a 6.2-liter engine gets about 20 miles per gallon. When it comes to driving fast, you always need to know where the nearest gas station is.

1C, 2A, 3E, 4B, 5D

Have your camera ready, because if you are cruising by any of these sights in a homegrown supercar, they're going to go by fast!

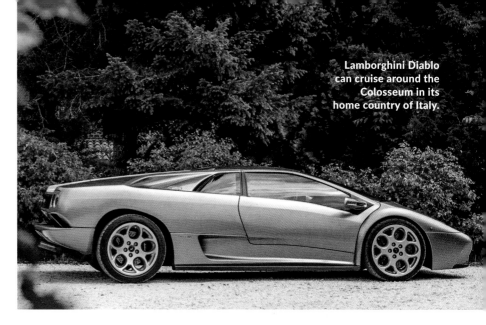

Lamborghini Diablo can cruise around the Colosseum in its home country of Italy.

The Hennessey Venom is at home on the streets of New York in its home country, the United States.

Say "Au revoir!" to the Citroën GT as it zips past the Eiffel Tower in its home country of France.

The Rolls-Royce Ghost, from England, looks very regal parked by Big Ben.

The Nissan GT-R is fit for royalty pulling up to the Tokyo Imperial Palace in Japan.

B. MERCEDES-BENZ In 2022, a 1955 Mercedes-Benz 300 SLR Uhlenhaut Coupe sold for the record-breaking sum of $143 million. Why? Well, it is really nice and extremely rare—one of only two prototypes that were ever made. (A prototype is a one-of-a-kind test model made to see if a new design idea works.) Mercedes-Benz said proceeds from the sale would fund a scholarship program for students studying environmental science. Save the planet! (But not the cash of whoever bought this beauty!)

WHAT DOES A "SLAMMED" CAR MEAN?

A. It is under a pile in a junkyard.

B. It has been customized to sit lower to the ground.

C. Braun Strowman body-slammed it.

QUESTION 24

Why will you never be picked up to ride in a Lamborghini Egoista?

A. It has never left the Lamborghini factory.

B. It is only used for food deliveries.

C. It only has one seat.

QUESTION 25

There was nothing cool about the Citroën B2 10 HP model K1 made in 1922. Why not?

A. It was powered by 1000 burning candles.

B. The air conditioner didn't work.

C. It was the first vehicle to drive across the Sahara Desert.

QUESTION 26

VS.

WHO WOULD WIN IN A RACE?

Michael Phelps vs. Sea Turtle

Connect the car-collecting celeb to one of their prized vehicles.

1. Lady Gaga

2. Beyoncé

3. The Rock

4. Kevin Hart

5. John Cena

A. Ferrari LaFerrari

B. 1970 Chevrolet El Camino

C. 2006 Rolls-Royce Phantom

D. 2010 Bugatti Veyron Grand Sport

E. 1969 Plymouth Road Runner

Which of these is not the name of a Lotus model? (Hint: Look for the pattern.)

ELEVEN	ELITE	ELETRE	ECLAT	ESPRIT	EXIGE	EVIJA
EMIRA	ELAN	EUROPA	EXCEL	ELISE	EVORA	ZIPPY

C. It only has one seat.

The Italian word *egoista* means "selfish" in English, and it is a fitting name. The car has a monster engine that puts out 600 horses and hits a top speed of 202 mph—but there is no passenger seat. This is a high-speed party for one!

ANSWER 26

Michael Phelps is the most decorated Olympian of all time with 28 medals. But sorry Mikey, this is one race you aren't going to win. In his peak condition, Phelps paddled across pools at 5.5 mph, while a leatherback sea turtle can hit speeds of 22 mph without ever working out. But if Phelps really wants to win, we suggest he turn it into a beach-running race—the same turtle shuffles along the sand at a top speed of 3 mph.

ANSWER 25

C. It was the first vehicle to drive across the Sahara Desert.

Company founder André Citroën initiated the expedition as he wanted to publicize his car company; he sent two of his buddies to actually carry out the mission for him. Hope they brought sunglasses.

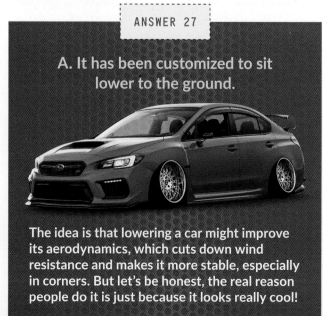

ANSWER 27

A. It has been customized to sit lower to the ground.

The idea is that lowering a car might improve its aerodynamics, which cuts down wind resistance and makes it more stable, especially in corners. But let's be honest, the real reason people do it is just because it looks really cool!

FAST AND FABULOUS FACTS

1B, 2D, 3A, 4E, 5C

Learn from these celebrities: If you want to have an amazing car collection, all you need to do is become one of the most famous entertainers in the world. Easy!

FERRARI LAFERRARI
Ferrari's most extreme performance design ever.

1970 CHEVROLET EL CAMINO
A muscle car with a pickup-truck rear!

2006 ROLLS-ROYCE PHANTOM
Considered the ultimate in fancy-schmancy luxury.

2010 BUGATTI VEYRON GRAND SPORT
Easily hits 200 mph, so go easy on that gas pedal!

Seriously Silly Question

DO BIRDS POOP ON CARS ON PURPOSE?

Don't take it personally—but yes, there's a chance that the gross white blob on your windshield was a well-aimed direct hit. Birds, like many animals, mark their territory with, um . . . stuff. So if your car is parked under a tree or in a garage near a nest for an extended period, this is a bird's yucky way of telling other birdies, "Keep off, that's mine!"

1969 PLYMOUTH ROAD RUNNER
Sorta plain looking on the outside with a beast of a powerful engine under the hood.

ZIPPY Notice the pattern? Yes, since the Eleven, almost all Lotus model names start with an "E." The Cortina, Seven, and Type 135 are exceptions to the rule, which is quite extraordinary!

CHAPTER THREE

SPEED SAGA

Quiz yourself on the history of vroom-vrooms.

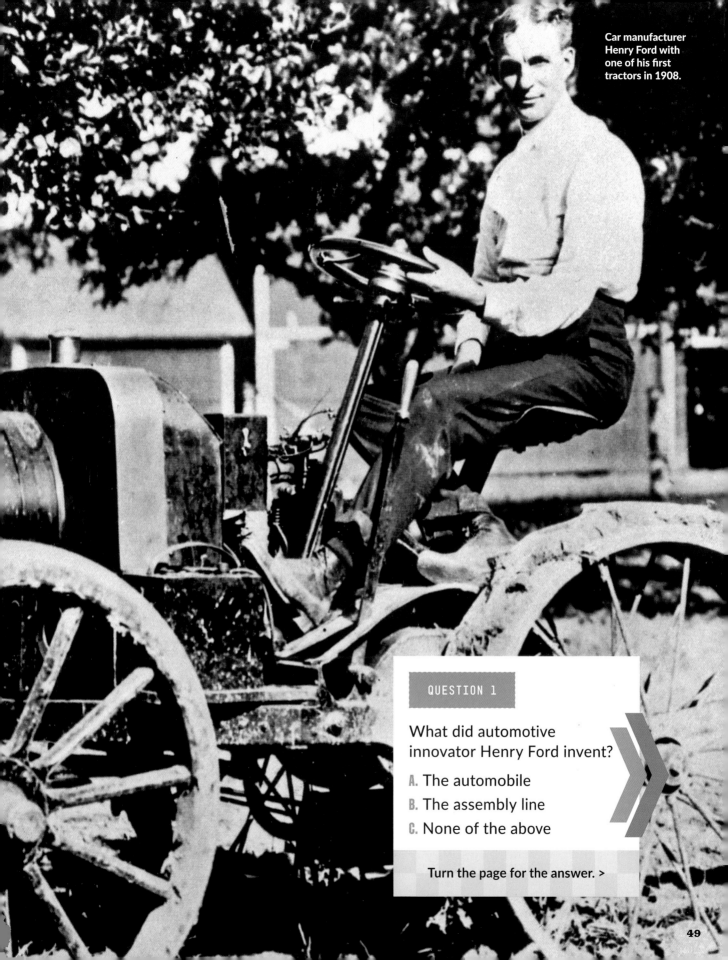

Car manufacturer Henry Ford with one of his first tractors in 1908.

QUESTION 1

What did automotive innovator Henry Ford invent?

A. The automobile
B. The assembly line
C. None of the above

Turn the page for the answer. >

ANSWER 1

C. None of the above

Henry Ford didn't invent the assembly line, but, man, did he know how to use it. Cars used to take a loooong time to build, but the assembly line simplified the process. Ford factory workers were able to build his Ford Model T quickly and cheaply, and they built lots of them! So many Model Ts were made— more than 15 million!—that Ford once said, "There's no use trying to pass a Ford, because there's always another one just ahead."

WHO MADE THE FIRST CAR?
Inventor Nicolas-Joseph Cugnot is credited with building the first self-propelled vehicle—a three-wheel tractor— for the French army in 1769.

QUESTION 2

Believe it or not, cars didn't always have air conditioning. (They were literally hot wheels!) What year were shoppers finally able to buy a "cool" car?

A. 1912

B. 1940

C. 2010

1. Made motorized bicycles

2. Was a shipping firm with steamships

3. Built farm tractors

4. Made lawnmowers

Turn the page for the answer. >

QUESTION 3

Match the legendary company to what it did before it made cars.

A. Honda

B. Lamborghini

C. Mitsubishi

D. Land Rover

QUESTION 4

What was the first year a person could make a telephone call from their car?

A. 1946 B. 1984 C. 2013

QUESTION 5

TRUE OR FALSE? Mercedes-Benz adapted its logo to symbolize peace after World War I ended.

B. 1940

In 1940, Packard became the first carmaker to offer factory-installed air conditioning in its rides. *Ahhhh*. Previous attempts to make long drives not so hot and sweaty included the Knapp Limo-Sedan Fan, an electric fan mounted inside a car. (So, even with your windows rolled up, you could still have your hat blow off your head.)

Ferruccio Lamborghini poses with two Lamborghini vehicles in 1970.

ANSWER 3

1A, 2C, 3B, 4D

Imagine eating bread made from grains that were harvested by a Lamborghini—talk about fast food!

An engineer demonstrates how to make a call from the first car phone.

A. 1946

The first phone service for those on the move was demonstrated on June 17, 1946. Those initial telephones made for cars weighed 80 pounds, and the equipment basically took up the entire trunk. There's no way you could carry that mobile phone around in your pocket!

FALSE While it does look a lot like a peace symbol, Mercedes-Benz's logo has three points for another reason. Each represents a different environment—land, sea, and air—that the company planned to build unrivaled vehicles to drive, float, and fly in. While they have dabbled in airplane engines and speedboats, the point that represents land should be extra pointy because that's where this company really rocks.

BURP ALERT!

Which fast-food restaurant was the first to feature a drive-through?

A. McDonald's
B. In-N-Out Burger
C. Krusty Burger

QUESTION 7

When was the first EV made?

A. 1973   B. 1832   C. 10,000 BCE

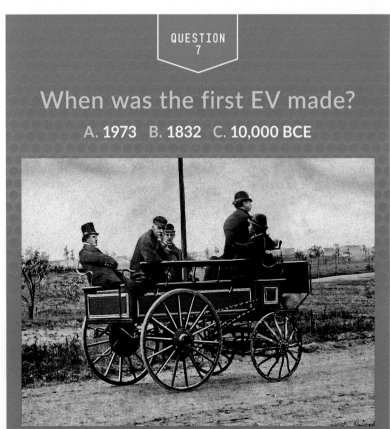

QUESTION 8

Driving sure makes you thirsty. What year was the built-in cupholder invented?

A. 1950   B. 1983   C. 2020

The first gas station in America opened in 1905. Before that, where did people go to refill their rides?

A. At natural-gasoline lakes

B. Pharmacies

C. Nowhere (when they ran out of gas, they threw out the car and bought a new one)

Which of these historic events happened first?

A. The first powered flight
B. The first recorded motor-car race
C. The first landing of humans on the moon

Let's go dinosaur hunting!

Five of these six car brands are extinct. Yes, you might still see old models of theirs on the road, but they're no longer being made. Can you pick out the five car brands that went the way of T. rex?

A. Saab
B. DeLorean
C. Saturn

D. Pontiac
E. Oldsmobile
F. Fiat

ANSWER 6

B. In-N-Out

A local chain of fast-food joints in Texas called the Pig Stand is believed to be the first to allow diners to stay in their cars while ordering grub back in 1921, but California-based In-N-Out was the first to have the kind of intercom ordering system we know today. Built in 1948, the burger shack had a sign promising "NO DELAY." It's a good thing they had the sign, because you usually can barely understand a word that comes out of those intercoms.

ANSWER 7

B. 1832

No, cavemen didn't ride around in battery-powered cars, but Robert Anderson, a Scottish inventor, did. He is credited with building the first "electric horseless carriage" sometime between 1832 and 1839. Shocking, isn't it?

ANSWER 9

B. Pharmacies

Hopefully the pharmacist never got confused and poured cough medicine into the tank!

ANSWER 8

B. 1983

There were many other ideas along the way, like cupholders that clipped on to windows and serving trays hidden in glove compartments, but it wasn't until 1983 that everyday cars got cupholders. Cheers to the Dodge Caravan and Plymouth Voyager, the first to give us a better place to put our drinks than our laps!

FILL 'ER UP NAME GAME

Here's what gas stations are called in different countries.

GAS BAR
(Canada)

SERVO
(Australia)

PETROL STATION
(U.K.)

GASOLINE STAND
(Japan)

THESE BRANDS ARE EXTINCT.

A. SAAB

B. DELOREAN

C. SATURN

D. PONTIAC

E. OLDSMOBILE

ANSWER 10

B. The first recorded motor-car race

Okay, being that this is a book about car trivia, that one might have been easy to guess. In 1895, the first recorded car race had competitors in France racing from Paris to Bordeaux and back. The winner's average speed? 15 mph. (If you're wondering, the Wright brothers took the first powered flight in 1903, and the moon landing was in 1969.)

If you see one in a parking lot, don't be afraid. Unlike the dinos in *Jurassic Park*, Saabs have no interest in eating you.

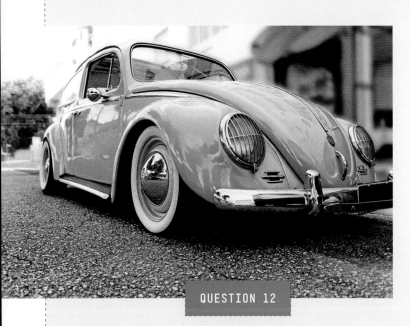

Volkswagen Beetle is this car's official name in Germany, but it has varying pet names in different countries—all having to do with its signature rounded shape.

Can you guess what nickname goes with which nation?

A. Bug

B. Frog

C. Turtle

D. Ladybug

1. Thailand

2. United States

3. France

4. Indonesia

QUESTION 13

WHICH CAME FIRST:
Matchbox or Hot Wheels?

QUESTION 14

CADILLAC IS NAMED AFTER:

A. Some guy from France

B. A constellation

C. A kind of frog that can hop really fast

Baker (right) shakes hands with comedian Lloyd Hamilton in 1900.

From the early 1900s to the 1940s, daredevil speedster Erwin G. Baker earned the name "Cannon Ball" for his many incredible feats. Which of these is the only record he didn't set during his lifetime?

A. Fastest drive across America on a motorcycle (11½ days)

B. The "Three Flags record" for "touching" three countries—Canada, the U.S., and Mexico—in three days on his motorcycle

C. Wettest drive—2300 miles on the riverbed of the Mississippi

Which car company was started first?

A. Ford

B. Honda

C. Mercedes-Benz

1C, 2A, 3D, 4B

Weirdly, for the first 30 years of its life, the Beetle was not called the Beetle at all. The car was created in 1938 and had a few different names until 1968, when brochures started referring to it as Käfer, German for "beetle."

CRAZY COLLECTIBLE

The most valuable Hot Wheels car that collectors could ever imagine owning is a 1969 pink rear-loading Beach Bomb. It's worth $175,000! But why is a toy car more valuable than many a real sports car? The toy's awkward design made it flip off Hot Wheels tracks, so the company scrapped the toy after making only a handful of prototypes in various colors. Only two pink Beach Bombs are known to exist, making them super rare. The lesson here? If you ever invent something that doesn't work, just wait a few decades—it might be worth $100K or more!

ANSWER 13 — **MATCHBOX**

In 1952, the school that English toy-maker Jack Odell's daughter attended had a rule that students could only bring in toys that fit inside a matchbox. Inspired, Odell created a line of mini toy cars called Matchbox. The little cars hit it big in America in 1968, when Mattel, the company that made Matchbox cars, decided that they shouldn't just look cool, they should also go really fast. Good idea!

Le Vroom!

ANSWER 14

A. Some guy from France

Antoine de la Mothe Cadillac was a Frenchman who, in 1701, established a settlement that became Detroit. When the car company Cadillac was founded in Detroit in 1902, they named it after ol' Antoine. *Le vroom, vroom!*

ANSWER 15

C. Wettest drive

Unless he had a really long snorkel, riding a motorcycle underwater is pretty impossible. Cannon Ball didn't only shine while riding motorcycles—he also competed in the 1922 Indy 500 and was the first commissioner of NASCAR.

ANSWER 16

C. Mercedes-Benz

Karl Benz founded the company that eventually became Mercedes-Benz in 1883. Ford came along in 1903, and Honda was the slowest to the car party, starting its business in 1948.

A collection of cars from Mercedes-Benz Classic

QUESTION 17

A "barn find" is:

A. A cow patty you accidentally just stepped in

B. Something that gets stuck in the treads of a farm tractor's tires

C. A supercool, super-old car that has been sitting in really any kind of aged structure, forgotten for decades

QUESTION 18

La Marquise is the world's oldest operating car. What can you use to fuel its engine?

A. Wood

B. Coal

C. Paper

D. All of the above

HONK!

Since 1921, a company called Bosch has been making horns for most of the major car companies, now ranging from BMW and Honda to Subaru and Porsche. Bosch says its horns' sound levels measure 110 decibels from six feet in front of a vehicle. What's that equal to in loudness?

A. Jackhammer

B. Thunderclap

C. Baby giggling

QUESTION 20

In what decade was the first bumper sticker stuck on a bumper?

A. The 1940s

B. The 1950s

C. 8000 BCE

QUESTION 21

Who was the first U.S. president to ride in a car?

A. George Washington
B. William McKinley
C. Abraham Lincoln

QUESTION 22

Visitors to Santo Island in Vanuatu, a South Pacific Ocean country, can see an incredible collection of WWII military vehicles at a spot called Million Dollar Point. If you want to see it, what will you need to bring?

A. A good pair of hiking boots
B. Binoculars
C. A scuba tank

QUESTION 23

BEFORE STEERING wheels were invented in the late 1800s, how did drivers steer cars?

A. By leaning in the direction they wanted the car to go.

B. They didn't—all roads were straight back then.

C. They used a lever called a tiller.

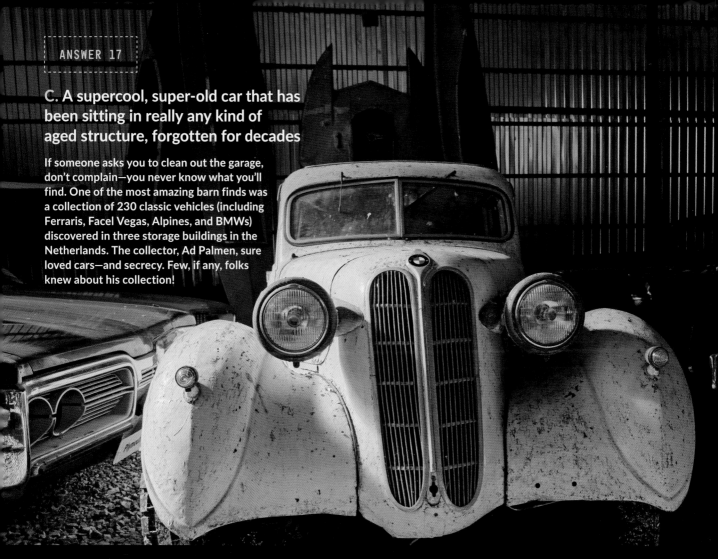

C. A supercool, super-old car that has been sitting in really any kind of aged structure, forgotten for decades

If someone asks you to clean out the garage, don't complain—you never know what you'll find. One of the most amazing barn finds was a collection of 230 classic vehicles (including Ferraris, Facel Vegas, Alpines, and BMWs) discovered in three storage buildings in the Netherlands. The collector, Ad Palmen, sure loved cars—and secrecy. Few, if any, folks knew about his collection!

POPULAR NICKNAMES FOR RUSTY RIDES

BANGER   BEATER   JALOPY   HEAP   RUST BUCKET   WRECK   CLUNKER

D. All of the above

La Marquise was made in France in 1884. It has a steam-powered engine, so it needs to burn materials to create steam to get the engine parts turning and the car moving. Speaking of moving, it takes about 30 minutes to heat up, but once it does, La Marquise can reach a top speed of 38 mph. (Impressive for a car that's well over 100 years old!)

A. JACKHAMMER

There are actually laws that say how loud a safe honker should be. In California, the law says a horn should be able to be heard at "a distance of not less than 200 feet," and in New York, horns can't be "unnecessarily loud or harsh." Guess that's why horns beep and don't scream "Get outta the way!"

A. The 1940s

Forest Gill, the owner of a Kansas City, Missouri, print shop, is credited with making the first bumper sticker. He noticed that people wrote messages on cardboard rectangles and tied them to their bumpers and thought there had to be a better, longer-lasting way to get their moving thoughts across. So he found some self-adhesive paper, and the rest is history. The message he wrote on the first bumper sticker? "Jones for Sheriff." No word on if Jones won, but the bumper-sticker fad sure did!

BUMPER'S GREATEST HITS Here are some of the most popular bumper stickers ever stuck.

ANSWER 21

B. William McKinley

America's 25th president, who served from 1897 to 1901, was the first to ride in a car—and, apparently, he didn't like it very much. The car was a Stanley Steamer, a steam-powered ride invented by O.F. Stanley. Stanley assured the president that cars were the way of the future, but McKinley didn't agree, saying, "Stanley's overoptimistic, I think, when he says those things will someday replace horses."

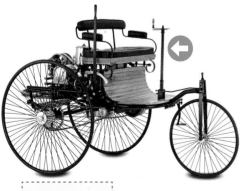

ANSWER 23

C. THEY USED A LEVER CALLED A TILLER. Inventor Alexander Winton is believed to be the first person to put a steering wheel in a car back in 1898. Before that, drivers would push and pull on a tiller, which changed the direction of the wheels in kind of the same way that a rudder works to steer a boat. We're getting seasick just thinking about it.

ANSWER 22

C. A scuba tank

After WWII, the U.S. Army didn't want to take all of their trucks, guns, and supplies back home and offered them to the French and British armies—for a price. But when the French and British balked, the Army was like "Okay, watch this!" and just dumped it all into the sea. Over the years, this site called Million Dollar Point has developed into an artificial reef, teeming with sea life. Do you think fish have pretend tank battles when no one is looking?

How many cars were involved
in the worst traffic
jam in recorded history?

A. 180   B. 1800   C. 18 million

In 1934, Chevrolet sponsored a downhill race for kid drivers to compete in using homemade vehicles powered by gravity. What is this type of race called?

A. Gravity Games
B. Soap Box Derby
C. Skinned-Knee Prix

In 1933, businessman Richard Hollingshead advertised his latest gimmick. It was a place where "the whole family is welcome, regardless of how noisy the children are." What was he talking about?

A. The first playground
B. The first drive-in movie theater
C. The first junkyard

QUESTION 27

Why was the 1969
Dodge Charger
Daytona banned from
racing in NASCAR?

A. It was too slow.
B. It was too fast.
C. It kept falling apart.

QUESTION 28

VS.

WHO WOULD WIN IN A RACE?

Lunar Roving Vehicle vs.
Mars Perseverance Rover

ANSWER 24

ARE YOU DERBY READY?
If you are between seven and 20 years old, you are allowed to take part in all of the fun! Go to soapboxderby.org to see all of the rules, find local race schedules, and get instructions on how to build (or buy) your own racer. Good luck!

B. Soap Box Derby

In 1933, a photographer named Myron Scott organized a competition for kids in Dayton, Ohio, where they raced in homemade cars built with orange crates and soap boxes, wagon and baby-carriage wheels, and anything else they found lying around. Chevrolet was so impressed by the race that the next year it became the first official sponsor of the All-American Soap Box Derby.

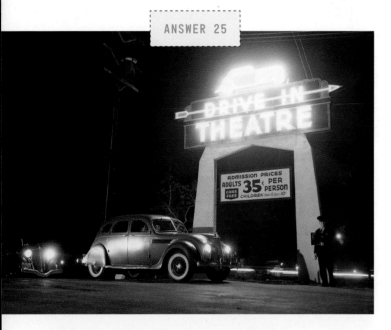

ANSWER 25

B. The first drive-in movie theater

Historians say that drive-in movie theaters existed as far back as the 1910s, but Hollingshead was the first to patent the concept, from how the cars were arranged to the sound system used. Drive-ins became very popular in the 1950s and '60s, with about 4000 drive-in theaters scattered around the country. Today there are more than 300 still operating, which you can find on authenticdriveins.com. No honking during the previews, please!

ANSWER 26

C. 18 million

The Guinness World Records reports that on April 12, 1990, this bumper-to-bumper mega-mess engulfed the East-West German border. The cause? It was Easter weekend, and Germans were excited to visit relatives and parts of the country previously off limits before the fall of the Berlin Wall just a few months earlier. Talk about worth the wait!

ANSWER 27

B. It was too fast.

During the 1969 and 1970 seasons, the Charger, with its huge rear wing and crazy nose cone, won tons of races. NASCAR basically said it wasn't fair that the Charger's design allowed it to soar past a then-unheard-of 200 mph—and the competition—so the sanctioning body banned this bad boy from its tracks.

The winner of our out-of-this-world race would be . . .

the Lunar Roving Vehicle! First used on the Apollo 15 mission in 1971, the LRV could go 8 mph, but the Moon's uneven surface had cautious astronauts cruising at 5 to 6 mph. As for the Perseverance rover on Mars? Well, it has a ton of incredible capabilities, such as collecting rock samples and taking space selfies, but speed isn't one of them. On hard-packed, flat ground, it crawls along at a little less than 0.1 mph.

Woof!

WHY DO DOGS STICK THEIR HEADS OUT OF CAR WINDOWS?

Seriously Silly Question

If your car has a canine passenger, that cute furry face is guaranteed to peek out from a rolled-down window the first chance it gets. What's up with that? Do dogs think that their ears look stylish when they're blowing backward?

Many experts believe it has to do with a doggy's sniffer. Dogs have much more sensitive noses than humans that they use to explore the world around them. Jennifer Cattet, Ph.D., an animal-behavior researcher, told *Discover* magazine, "When sticking their head out the window, they can smell every person in the street, every trash can they go by, every patch of grass, restaurant, and other dogs. It's like watching TV for us." Dogs sure love a show that stinks!

CHAPTER FOUR

SPORTS AND STUNTS

On your mark,
get set—answer!

QUESTION 1

Daredevil Evel Knievel's first public motorcycle jump didn't include a perfect landing. What did he hit as he landed?

A. A bus

B. A box of rattlesnakes

C. His butt

Turn the page for the answer. >

Evel Knievel makes a jump over 13 buses at Wembly Stadium in London in May 1975, and . . .

ANSWER 1

B. A box of rattlesnakes

. . . he lands it! (But breaks a bone in the process.)

Robert Craig Knievel Jr. was always getting into trouble growing up, eventually earning the nickname Evel (pronounced "evil") after landing in jail for crashing his motorcycle while trying to evade police. The rest, as they say, is history, with Evel turning his love of risk-taking into a career and becoming one of the most famous stunt performers in the world during the 1970s.

The stunts started in 1965 when Evel decided to put on his first show to help support his family. He sold tickets to the event, promising a jump over two caged mountain lions and a box of rattlesnakes. Evel cleared the lions, but his 350cc Honda clipped the 20-foot-long box of

rattlesnakes. He wobbled but somehow managed to stay on his bike, and the crowd went wild.

Dressed in star-spangled outfits, Evel built a career on wildly dangerous and often-unsuccessful jumps. Before huge crowds, he launched himself over the fountains at Caesars Palace in Las Vegas on a 650cc Triumph Bonneville T120 but crashed; nearly flew over 13 parked buses at London's Wembley Stadium on a Harley-Davidson XR-750 but hit the last bus and crashed; and tried to jump across Idaho's Snake River Canyon in his custom-built, steam-powered Skycycle X-2 but—you guessed it—came up short, with the rocket crashing into the canyon below. At least it had a parachute!

FAST FACT The CC in 350cc stands for cubic capacity, which refers to the amount of fuel and air an engine can hold. The higher the number, the more powerful the engine.

COOL!

LOOK OUT BELOW

Peep some of Evel's most famous rides.

350cc Honda

650cc Triumph T120 Bonneville

Harley Davidson XR-750

Evel Knievel
attempts to jump
Snake River
Canyon in Idaho
in 1974.

FAST FACT

Evel performed many other stunts over his career and, by the time he retired, held the Guinness world record for the most bones broken in a lifetime. We don't recommend trying to, well, break it—Evel broke 433 bones! Considering there are 206 bones in the human body, that means he had a ton of repeat snaps.

QUESTION 2

Formula 1 driver Ernst Loof has a record that no one is hoping to beat. Can you guess what it is?

A. Most flat tires in a race

B. Shortest driving career

C. Worst taste in driving music

D. Most pit-stop snack breaks

SPOT THE SPONSOR

Companies can pay to put their logos on race cars and drivers' uniforms. This is called sponsoring a team. Can you spot the fake sponsor in these photos?

A. Domino's car

B. Huggies Diapers car

C. Swiffer car

D. No fakers here, folks

QUESTION 3

In 1997, the vehicle in this photo broke the land-speed record, jetting 763.035 mph across Nevada's Black Rock Desert.

What was it named?

A. ThrustSSC   B. Fasty McFastface   C. Red Bull Rocket

Cars line up to race in Darwin, Australia, in October 2019.

Turn the page for the answer. >

QUESTION 5

Who was the first female driver to compete in both the Daytona 500 and the Indy 500?

A. Danica Patrick
B. Janet Guthrie
C. Simona de Silvestro

QUESTION 6

These vehicles are competing in an annual race across Australia. What are they all powered by?

A. Diesel
B. Vegemite
C. The sun
D. Kangaroo poop

QUESTION 7

Which team has the most Formula 1 (F1) championships?

A. Ferrari
B. Lotus
C. Red Bull

ANSWER 2

B. Shortest driving career

When it was time for racers to go at the 1953 German Grand Prix, Loof hit the gas and his Veritas raced just six and a half feet from the start line before its fuel pump died and the car came to a stop (and with it, his career as an F1 racer).

Ferrari cars in the paddock before the 1953 German Grand Prix

ANSWER 4

D. No fakers here, folks

While there certainly are a lot of accidents that occur during NASCAR races, they're not the kind that a diaper would be able to help much with!

ANSWER 3

A. ThrustSSC

While we think Fasty McFastface is a much catchier name, this insane machine was dubbed ThrustSSC. "SSC" stands for SuperSonic Car. It's the fastest car in the world (as of the time this book was published). Besides breaking the land-speed record, it was also the first land vehicle to break the sound barrier. That means if the car sped by you, it'd take a few seconds after it passed for you to hear the driver screaming, "Where are the brakes on this thing?!"

HOW DO YOU BREAK THE SOUND BARRIER?
Sound travels in waves through the atmosphere. The speed of sound can vary depending on conditions, but generally speaking it moves about 760 mph at sea level. So if you want to make a joke in class, just run more than 760 mph, and you'll be gone before your teacher hears it.

ANSWER 5 ## B. Janet Guthrie

At the start of 1977's Indy 500, track owner Tony Hulman altered his famous loudspeaker announcement to mark the historic occasion, saying, "In company with the first lady ever to qualify at Indianapolis, gentlemen start your engines!" The lady he was speaking of was Janet Guthrie, whom the press called "The Goddess of Racing." Guthrie was the first woman to compete at Indy, as well as in the Daytona 500 that same year. "I'm a driver who happens to be a woman," she told a reporter in 1976. "There is no reason—physical, emotional, or psychological—that a woman cannot drive a car as well as a man."

ANSWER 6

C. The Sun

The Bridgestone World Solar Challenge has been whipping across Australia for over 30 years, challenging car designers to make fast and powerful vehicles fueled only by that great big glowing orb in the sky. The race is nearly 1900 miles long from the top of Australia to the bottom. Bring your love of adventure (and lots of sunscreen) if you plan on racing.

ANSWER 7 ## A. Ferrari

As of 2023, Ferrari has 16 constructors' (another term for team) championships, with Williams a distant second at nine and Mercedes and McLaren tied for third with eight apiece (keep up, slowpokes!).

While Ferrari is obviously very good at making very fast race cars, it has one big advantage when it comes to total crowns: These folks have been at it longer than the other teams! Ferrari is the longest-serving squad in Formula 1, having revved its engines since the first F1 season in 1950.

POLE POSITION
In addition to having the most constructors' championships, Team Ferrari also has the highest number of individual drivers' world championships at 15.

QUESTION 8

The Daytona 500 has been run at Daytona International Speedway in Florida since 1959. Before that, at what unlikely place was the event that would become known as "The Great American Race" held?

A. **The beach**

B. **Around the Enchanted Castle at Disney World**

C. **The Indy 500 track (ultimate loaner!)**

D. **A supermarket parking lot**

Racers start the pace lap before the 2023 Daytona 500.

WHAT IS A TRI-OVAL?
The shape of Daytona's track is kind of like a triangle with rounded edges. Why? It was the only way the track designer could fit it in the space.

QUESTION 9

Besides a trophy, what odd thing is the winner of the Indy 500 handed after they cross the finish line?

A. **A single rose**

B. **A batch of freshly made cookies**

C. **A bottle of milk**

QUESTION 10

GET IN SHAPE!

See if you can match the car to its proper track type.

1. NASCAR
2. F1 car
3. Drag racer

A.

B.

C.

Cars drive the Le Mans track before the 100th anniversary of the race in 2023.

QUESTION 11

The 24 Hours of Le Mans is a race in France where the car that covers the greatest distance in 24 hours on the track wins. In 1923, the Automobile Club de l'Ouest (ACO) held the first race in a town near Le Mans, France. Besides staying awake all night, the drivers faced another challenge. What was it?

A. A hailstorm

B. A gas shortage

C. Tires that kept popping as the asphalt got too hot

D. Too many chickens trying to cross the road

Turn the page for the answer. >

SOME LE RECORDS

1988
French driver Roger Dorchy hits fastest track speed, 253 mph.

2010
Audi R15 TDI completes 397 laps in 24 hours, the most in race history.

2017
Driver Kamui Kobayashi scores the highest average lap speed of 157 mph.

2022
16-year-old Josh Pierson is the youngest driver to start a race.

ANSWER 8

A. The beach

Daytona Beach, Florida, is known as "the birthplace of speed" because, in 1903, two guys decided to race their cars on the beach's packed sand. The racecourse eventually expanded to include both the beach and the streets of the city of Daytona and finally moved to its permanent home when Daytona International Speedway opened. This was good news for racing fans who get an incredible view of the action in the stands—and even better news for sandcastles, which are no longer in danger of getting run over!

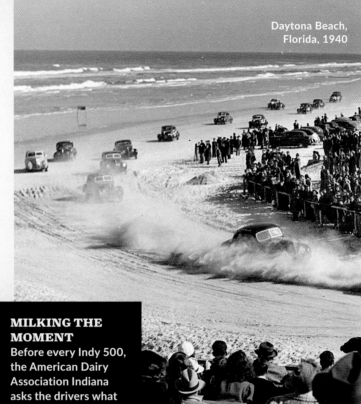

Daytona Beach, Florida, 1940

Driver Josef Newgarden celebrates his Indy 500 win in 2023.

MILKING THE MOMENT
Before every Indy 500, the American Dairy Association Indiana asks the drivers what their victory milk of choice would be. The options are whole, 2 percent, or skim, but drivers are allowed to write in choices like chocolate, strawberry, or (see below) buttermilk.

ANSWER 10

1C, 2B, 3A

Race cars are built to maximize speed on a track. F1 cars use rear wings, which help them grip the turns on a track like Nürburgring Nordschleife in Germany (track B) with more than 150 turns. NASCAR racers are built with monster engines and grippy tires that help them reach speeds of over 200 mph on the straightaways while hugging the turns on a track like Talladega (track C). Drag cars are built for straight speed—they don't need features to help them hug turns. They just need 12,000-hp engines to blast them down tracks like the Bristol Dragway (track A)!

ANSWER 9

C. A bottle of milk

If you've watched the ending of the Indy 500, you might have noticed this strange tradition: The victorious driver gets a bottle of ice-cold milk, which they usually sip before dumping over their heads. The tradition began in 1936, when three-time winner Louis Meyer was photographed holding up three fingers with one hand and a bottle of buttermilk with the other. He later explained that, when he was a kid, his mother told him cold milk would refresh him on a hot day. From 1947 and continuing through 1955, winners instead chose cold water served in a silver cup. But then the dairy industry offered a cash bonus in '56 if drivers got back on the milk wagon—and they did!

A car spins out during a heavy rain at Le Mans in 2023.

Wow!

ANSWER 11

A. A hailstorm

After 100 years of running the classic 24 Hours of Le Mans, racers can count on one thing at this grueling race: It almost always rains. But on that first running, Mother Nature decided to make things even more interesting by adding ice pellets to the drivers' worries. Gee, thanks!

The rules of Le Mans are simple: Teams of drivers compete to see how many laps their car can complete in 24 hours. Thirty-three cars started the first race in 1923, and 24 hours later, 30 made it across the finish line. Not bad! French auto manufacturer Chenard-Walcker won first place, with its team of drivers having covered 128 laps. Even more impressive numbers? In a tent set up to feed drivers taking a break during the race, 150 gallons of soup and 50 chickens were gobbled up.

QUESTION 12

What is the purpose of a drag-racing car's wheelie bar?

A.
It allows the car to do a supercool wheelie.

B.
It stops the car from doing a scary wheelie.

C.
It adds a backup wheel in case one pops during the race.

QUESTION 13

In 1908, the longest car race in history was run: The Great New York-to-Paris Auto Race.

Drivers started in New York City and drove across the country, then got their cars and themselves onto boats, sailed across the Pacific until they hit Asia and started driving again. Though the route changed many times and not everyone went the exact same way, the finish line was in Paris. Can you guess the time difference between the first-place finisher and the runner-up?

A. 3 seconds   C. 4 hours

B. 57 seconds   D. 26 days

WHAT SIGNAL STARTS WHICH RACE?

1. Formula 1

2. NASCAR

3. Drag race

A.
Waving green flag

B.
Vertical stand of colored lights

C.
Horizontal bank of lights switching off

Gumball 3000 racers in Times Square, New York

Turn the page for the answer. >

QUESTION 15

At the Brazilian Grand Prix in 2019, which crew recorded the fastest pit stop in Formula 1 history, changing out all four tires on a car in under two seconds? (Hint: Their company sponsor might have something to do with why the crew had so much energy.)

A. Ferrari
B. Red Bull
C. McLaren

QUESTION 16

The Gumball 3000 is a car rally where thousands of drivers and their hot rides take part in an epic race across multiple countries. What does the winner get?

A. $10 million
B. A lifetime supply of gumballs
C. Nothing

QUESTION 17

WHICH COSTS MORE?
A. The steering wheel of a Formula 1 car
B. A brand-new Chevrolet Camaro SS

B. It stops the car from doing a scary wheelie.

Since some dragster engines produce 12,000 horsepower that rocket the car to 330 mph in less than 4.0 seconds, the danger of the front wheels coming off the ground and the whole car flipping over is very real. (They call this a blow-over.) The bar protects the driver from having a giant car land on their head.

A dragster smokes the competition in Las Vegas, Nevada, in 2018.

WHAT'S UP WITH BURNOUTS?

Drag racers do burnouts (smoke their tires) before a race. Sure, it looks really awesome, but there are practical reasons as well. Cold tires are hard and don't grip the track well. Burnouts warm them up, which helps make them slightly softer and gain more traction because more of the tire is mushed down and making contact with the road. And burnouts also burn off any materials (like debris or oil) that may have gotten on the tires while the car was rolling into racing position.

The New York City starting line of the New York–to–Paris race on February 12, 1908.

D. 26 days

The longest car race in history also has the biggest gap between the first- and second-place time in history. The winner of this bonkers race was the American team of Monty Roberts and George Schuster, who completed the course in 169 days in a 1907 Thomas Flyer car. Out of six cars competing, only three were able to finish the 22,000-mile trek. A second event, dubbed the World Race, was held in 2011, and the 1907 Thomas Flyer was wheeled out of a museum to participate. Good to see you again, Thomas!

1C, 2A, 3B

FUN FACT!

The stand of lights used at drag races is called a Christmas Tree. What's the best present a driver can get under that tree? First place!

B. Red Bull

Not only did Red Bull Racing's Max Verstappen win the 2019 Brazilian Grand Prix, but his pit crew pulled off a record-breaking pit stop, servicing Verstappen's Honda-powered RB15 in an incredible 1.82 seconds. (That is the same amount of time it takes to blink your eyes five times!) And it wasn't just a lucky stop—the team beat its own record of 1.88 seconds that it had set at the German Grand Prix earlier that season.

Verstappen and members of the Red Bull team in Brazil a few years later in 2023

C. Nothing

The Gumball 3000 was started in 1999 by a businessperson named Maximillion Cooper and is more of a rolling party than a race. The 3000-mile event takes place over the course of a week, with daily check-in spots for drivers to relax, goof around, and show off their incredible rides—ranging from modern hypercars to more vintage cruisers. Drivers have included actors, car collectors, musicians, athletes, and everyone in between. Every year the course changes. So far it has taken place in North America, Europe, and the Middle East. The location may change, but the vibe is always the same. Gumball is not about how fast you can finish—it's about how much fun you have and how cool you look doing it.

A. THE STEERING WHEEL OF A FORMULA 1 CAR

The Red Bull team estimates that the steering wheel on an F1 car costs about $50,000. For comparison, an entire new Camaro costs about $40,000. And while $50K might seem like a lot for a steering wheel, it's not so much when you consider that the whole car will cost somewhere around $15 million! Why is the steering wheel so expensive? As you can see from all of those buttons and dials, it controls a little more than just turning right and left.

QUESTION 18

Formula E is a racing organization with Formula 1–style cars that are all electric. In 2020, the season was canceled due to the pandemic, so they held a special virtual race using high-tech race-car simulators. What was the shocking reason that driver Daniel Abt was disqualified after coming in third place?

A. He wasn't wearing a mask.

B. He crashed too much.

C. He didn't drive the car.

In most car races, vehicles go in a counter-clockwise direction.

Which direction do racers at the annual Pikes Peak run go?

F1 cars line up for the British Grand Prix in June 2006.

A.

B.

C.

QUESTION 19

What's the best position at the start of a car race called?

A. Cheat seat   B. Pole position   C. Speedy spot

A crew member checks wear on the tires during the NASCAR Cup Series Coca-Cola 600 in May 2023.

Turn the page for the answer. >

QUESTION 21

A Funny Car is:

A. Something clowns drive

B. A special NASCAR vehicle with jokes painted on the side to entertain fans

C. A drag-racing vehicle

D. A car that's a little off-balance

QUESTION 22

What is a "slingshot" in race-car driving?

A. A weapon drivers use to fling pebbles at their competitors

B. A racing maneuver that uses airflow to suddenly propel a car forward

C. The name of a super-sugary energy drink drivers gulp down during pit stops

QUESTION 23

HOW MANY SETS of tires do NASCAR cars go through during the Daytona 500?

A. 2
B. 4
C. 8

ANSWER 18

C. He didn't drive the car.

When competitors noticed that Abt's face was blocked by equipment on the Zoom camera during the race and that he didn't participate in any interviews afterward, they realized that Abt wasn't actually behind the wheel of his racing-simulator cockpit. Instead, he got professional simulation racer Lorenz Hoerzing to take his place. Can you imagine hiring someone else to play a video game for you?

A driver demonstrates a racing simulator.

WHY DO THEY CALL IT THE POLE POSITION?

The name comes from a different type of racing—horse racing. Like with cars, the horse with the best qualifying time would get to start in the front and on the inside, right next to the pole of the inside fence of the track. Giddyup!

The start of the 1999 Australian Grand Prix

ANSWER 20

↑

A. Up

The nickname of this event—the Race to the Clouds—kind of gives it away. The Pikes Peak International Hill Climb is a contest to see which driver can climb to the summit of Pikes Peak in Colorado the fastest. The course that winds up the mountain is 12.42 miles long and features 156 turns, and the finish line is 14,115 feet high. Don't look down!

ANSWER 19

B. Pole position

The pole position of a race is at the front of the racing pack, on the inside lane of the track. It's the spot that puts a driver in the best position to win because it creates the shortest distance around the track. The driver who gets the pole position had the fastest qualifying time in the trials before the race.

Wait, so the fastest driver gets the best spot? Isn't that like giving LeBron James rocket-powered sneakers when he can already dunk over everyone? Sort of. But someone has to get that spot, and racing to see who it is makes the most sense, right? You can't have a bunch of Formula 1 teams flipping coins to nab it!

ANSWER 21

C. A drag-racing vehicle

When Francisco Hernandez, head of racing activities at Ford Motor Company's Lincoln-Mercury Division, saw this style of drag-racing car back in the 1960s, he remarked that it looked "funny." Decades later, the name has stuck. Funny Cars have carbon-fiber bodies that sort of look like those of regular street cars, but they are known to hit speeds well over 300 mph. Nothing funny about that!

FAST & FUNNIEST
In 2017, Driver Robert Hight hit a record-setting 339.87 mph rocketing down the 1000-foot track at Sonoma Raceway in his Chevrolet Camaro SS Funny Car. Apparently he was in a big rush to win!

ANSWER 22

B. A racing maneuver that uses airflow to suddenly propel a car forward

When a car is driving really close to the one in front of it (called drafting), it benefits from the lead car battling a lot of the wind resistance—the lead car pushes against the force of the wind, while the trailing car has smooth air to cruise in. Then when the second car quickly steers out of the draft, it breaks the air vacuum, which can provide a burst of speed, "slingshotting" the car ahead of the leader. See ya!

Even race cars like to snuggle.

ANSWER 23

C. 8 They might not use them all, but current rules allow a team to use eight sets of tires during the race—that breaks down to one set for qualifying and seven for the big show. Pretty pricey, when you realize that a single tire costs $500!

WHERE DO OLD TIRES GO WHEN THEY DIE?
If you've ever been on an artificial football or soccer field, you might have noticed tiny black rubber crumbles that kind of look like dirt on the turf. On many fields, those rubber pellets are diced up old tires. The crumbles provide extra padding for athletes running and falling on the turf. Wow, these tires have quite an exciting life—from driving in races to getting to play football!

Ken Block and Alex Gelsomino drive in a final at the ESPN X Games in August 2006.

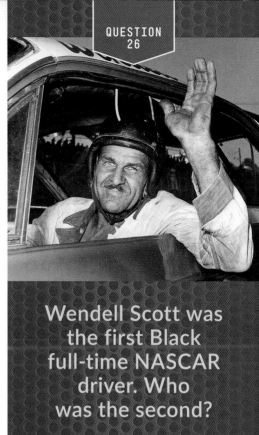

Wendell Scott was the first Black full-time NASCAR driver. Who was the second?

QUESTION 24

Ken Block was an incredible stunt and rally-car driver who made a series of incredible YouTube trick videos that have hundreds of millions of views.

What is the series called?

A. *Gymkhana*

B. *No Brakes Block*

C. *Ken You Believe How Fast I'm Driving?*

A. Micheal Jordon

QUESTION 25

VS.

WHAT WOULD WIN IN A RACE?

A fastball thrown by MLB star Shohei Ohtani vs. a Kia Sorento

B. Bubba Wallace

C. Lamar Jackson

Turn the page for the answer. >

QUESTION 27

The Indianapolis Motor Speedway track was once made up of millions of bricks. They have long since been paved over, except for one narrow strip, called the Yard of Bricks. What is the weird thing that winners of the Indy 500 and Brickyard 400 do at the Yard of Bricks?

A. Tap dance on it

B. Kiss it

C. Use a Swiffer to sweep up race debris

QUESTION 28

WHAT DOES RPM STAND FOR?

A. Revolutions per minute
B. Racing precise machine
C. Really puffy muffin

ANSWER 24

A. *Gymkhana*

The name Gymkhana comes from the 19th century term for horse competitions in India, where tricks and skills were put on display. Block took the name and applied it to the horsepower under the hood of his car. If you haven't seen any of the series, be sure to check out *Gymkhana 5*, where Block races through the streets of San Francisco, drifting between moving trolley cars. (It's way more awesome than it sounds.) Sadly, Block died in a snowmobile accident in January 2023. His skills and love of cars live on in his epic.

Block wins the Red Bull Global Rallycross in May 2015.

ANSWER 25

ANSWER 26

B. Bubba Wallace

In 2013, Darrell "Bubba" Wallace won his first NASCAR Truck Series race (that's a division where drivers race pickup trucks). With that win, Wallace became the first Black driver in 50 years to win in one of the association's top three national series. Who does he drive for now? 23XI Racing, the team co-owned by NBA Hall of Famer Michael Jordan.

In a 60-foot-6-inch race (the precise distance from the pitcher's mound to home plate), **Shohei's** fastball would win, and it isn't even close. His pitch can reach the plate at 100-plus mph in less than half a second. In a *Car and Driver* road test, a 2023 Kia Sorento took a whole 21.5 seconds to get up to 100 mph. Now, an important question regarding Shohei's fastball: Who do you think hates it more—the batter who is trying to hit it or the poor catcher who has to catch it? That's gotta hurt!

B. Kiss it

It all started in 1996. After winning the Brickyard 400, NASCAR legend Dale Jarrett and crew chief Todd Parrott kneeled down, puckered up, and smooched the Yard of Bricks. Yuck. The celebration has since become tradition—if you plan to win, then plan to get kissin'!

Pucker up!

Sure hope those bricks used breath mints this morning.

ANSWER 28

DASHBOARD DECODER

Many cars have a tachometer on the dashboard that shows an engine's rpm. It is measured in thousands, with revs getting higher the harder the driver steps on the accelerator pedal. When they shift gears, the revs go down and start to build again. The expression "flooring it!" means pushing the pedal all the way down to the floorboards.

x 1000 R/MIN

A. Revolutions per minute

As delicious as a puffy muffin sounds, the answer is all about revolutions—specifically how many times the engine's crankshaft makes one full rotation (turn) every minute. That's how a car gets its power and speed. An average car will be at around 1500 to 2000 rpm while cruising at 55 mph on a highway. Talk about revved up!

Seriously Silly Question

IF THEY BUILT A BRIDGE TO THE MOON, HOW LONG WOULD IT TAKE TO DRIVE THERE?

Pack a whole bunch of snacks because it this is going to be a very long road trip. The moon is about 238,900 miles away. If you drove 55 mph (gotta stay safe, right?) that would take 4344 hours. With 24 hours in a day, that's 181 days, which is about six months on the road. Remember to buckle up—space is weightless and you definitely don't want to float away before you get there!

CHAPTER FIVE

BIG, LOUD, AND WEIRD

Power through questions

about mighty machines.

Grave Digger during Monster Jam in Florida in August 2022

ANSWER 1

B. Highest jump off a ramp

Krysten Anderson (center) with drivers Bryan Wright (left) and Adam Anderson (right) in Las Vegas in 2018

In 2020, Anderson and Grave Digger earned the world record for highest jump off a ramp by a monster truck, soaring 33 feet, 9.6 inches into the air. Considering Grave Digger weighs 12,000 pounds, that could not have been a soft landing!

4 MONSTER-SIZE FACTS ABOUT GRAVE DIGGER

1 Even though it is a behemoth (12,000 pounds), it is able to accelerate faster than many superlight sports cars, going from a standstill to 30 mph in just 1.52 seconds!

2 ITS TIRES ARE 5½ FEET TALL, WITH EACH ONE WEIGHING ABOUT 850 POUNDS.

3 ITS ENGINE PUMPS OUT 1500 HORSEPOWER.

4 Grave Digger has two onboard fire extinguishers pointed at its engine in case things get too hot under the hood and it bursts into flames. Monster trucks rev up a lot of heat!

QUESTION 2

Trucks are classified as light-, medium-, or heavy-duty, depending on something called their GVWR. What does that stand for?

A. Gross vehicle weight rating

B. Gross vehicle, wash required

C. Gram volume watt ratio

PUT THE PASSENGER IN THEIR SPECIALIZED RIDE:

1. U.S. president
2. The Pope
3. Mr. Peanut

A.

B.

C.

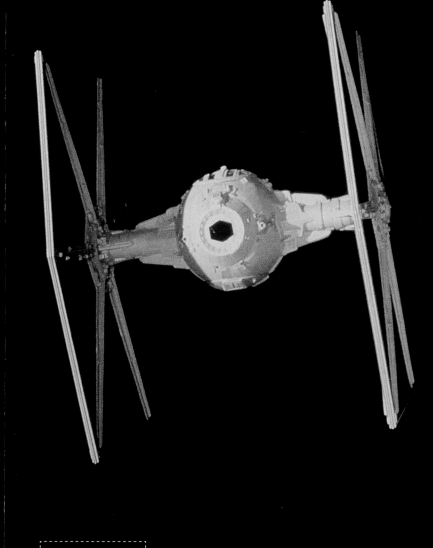

Turn the page for the answer. >

QUESTION 4

What kind of vehicle does SpongeBob SquarePants sometimes drive for work?

A. Fish Stick Shift

B. Patty Wagon

C. Stingray

QUESTION 5

Why won't Elon Musk, co-founder of the electric-car company Tesla, ever be able to drive his 2008 Roadster again?

A. The battery died.

B. It got stolen.

C. He blasted it into space.

QUESTION 6

Behind the scenes of the *Star Wars* movies, sound designer Ben Burtt got very creative when it came to inventing the noises we hear in the flicks, from the hum of lightsabers to Darth Vader's creepy breathing. For the TIE fighters, he overlaid two noises to make that signature screeching sound. What were they? (Pick two.)

A. A blender   B. Elephants   C. An attack helicopter   D. Cars driving on wet pavement

GVWR IN HIPPOS!

THE AVERAGE FEMALE HIPPO WEIGHS 3000 POUNDS.

2023 Ford F-150 (light), GVWR 7350 pounds—two hippos	School bus (medium), GVWR 26,000 pounds—eight hippos	Garbage truck (heavy), GVWR 33,000 pounds—11 hippos

ANSWER 2

A. Gross vehicle weight rating

That's a very fancy term that basically means how much weight a truck can safely carry. The GVWR is helpful to know if you are transporting a herd of hippos, for example, and you're not sure how many to take on each trip.

Pope Francis leaving the Vatican in the Popemobile, May 2023

AMAZING FACTS ABOUT THE BEAST

It weighs 15,000 pounds due to thick bulletproof windows and 8.0-inch bomb-resistant metal plating all around it.

It is equipped with weapons and a fire-fighting system in case anyone tries to attack it.

There are multiple identical Beasts (used in case one breaks down or if the Secret Service wants to use one as a decoy).

The Beast gets flown to any country the president will be visiting.

It has a mini-fridge stocked with a supply of the president's blood type in case of emergency. Do you think there's also room for drinks and snacks?

ANSWER 3   ## 1A, 2C, 3B

The Pope rides in the armor-protected Popemobile (yes, it is really called that!), the U.S. president rides in a special limousine nicknamed "the Beast," and the Planters mascot, Mr. Peanut, rides in the Nutmobile. It isn't bulletproof, but it would make a delicious mess if it crashed into a jelly factory.

B. Patty Wagon

As SpongeBob explains to his starfish friend Patrick, the Patty Wagon has a sesame-seed finish, pickle tires, and a grilled leather interior. Under the hood, there's a fuel-injected "french fryer" with dual-overhead grease traps. Before they take it out for a spin, Patrick worries that SpongeBob doesn't have a license, to which SpongeBob replies, "You don't need a license to drive a sandwich."

C. He blasted it into space.

In 2018, one of Musk's other companies, SpaceX, launched a Falcon Heavy rocket into space carrying a unique payload onboard: his red 2008 Tesla Roadster. The car and a spacesuit-wearing dummy named Starman are currently millions of miles away, circling the sun on a path that crosses the orbit of Mars.

Wha'?

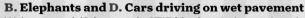

B. Elephants and D. Cars driving on wet pavement
Wait a second, if the sound of TIE (that's twin-ion engines, by the way) fighters was invented, does that mean that Baby Yoda also isn't real?!

QUESTION 7

Here's a championship that no one wants to win: Which is the most stolen vehicle in America?

A. Chevrolet pickup
B. Honda Accord
C. Nissan No Locks

QUESTION 8

WHAT IS THE WORLD SPEED RECORD FOR AN ELECTRIC DRAG CAR?

A. 100.5 mph
B. 157.2 mph
C. 202.82 mph

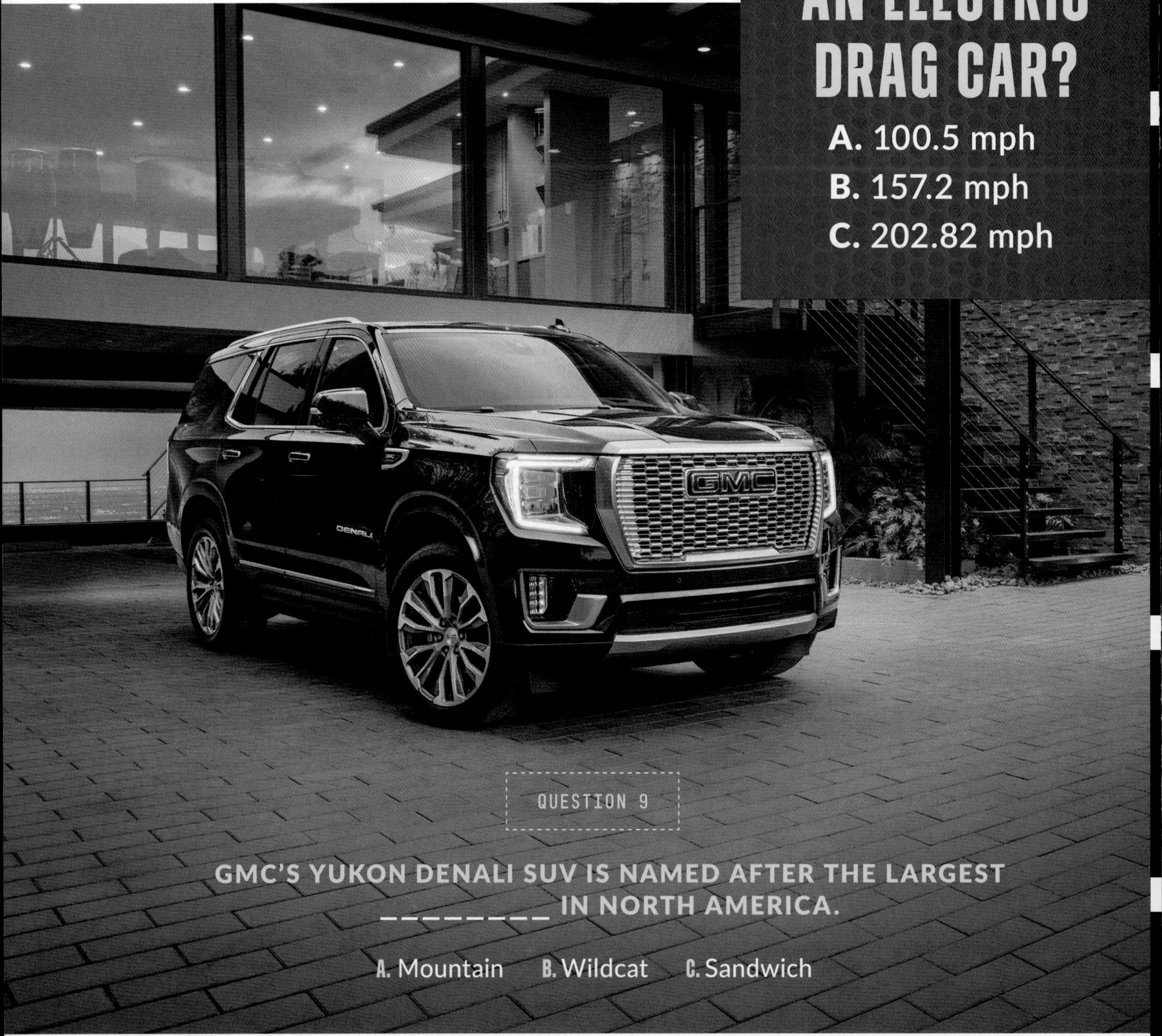

QUESTION 9

GMC'S YUKON DENALI SUV IS NAMED AFTER THE LARGEST _________ IN NORTH AMERICA.

A. Mountain B. Wildcat C. Sandwich

A

Two of these statements are famous urban legends (meaning they aren't true), and one is 100 percent true. Which is the real road story?

A.
The highest speeding ticket ever handed out was to someone driving a Koenigsegg CCR supercar at 242 mph in a 75-mph zone.

B.
The Chevy Nova sold poorly in South America because "nova" translates to "doesn't go" in Spanish.

C.
The first vehicle Henry Ford built, the Quadricycle, had a BIG problem: It was too large to roll out of the door of the shed he built it in.

B

C

WHAT IS A 4X4?

A.
A type of wood

B.
A truck with four wheels on each side

C.
A vehicle whose engine delivers power to all four wheels at once

ANSWER 7

A. Chevrolet pickup

The National Insurance Crime Bureau puts out an annual report titled "Hot Wheels." ("Hot," in this case, means stolen.) The 2022 report says that Chevy full-size pickups were the most wanted by car thieves, followed closely by Ford pickups. Um, congrats?

A. Mountain

Denali, also known as Mount McKinley, is the highest peak in North America, sticking out 20,310 feet above Alaska. Unfortunately, you can't ride to the top in the comfort of a GMC Denali—the only way up is to climb.

ANSWER 8 C. 202.82 mph

In 2022, driver Steve Huff broke the speed record for an electric dragster, beating his own record of 202.52 mph! (Wonder if he was, uh, mad at himself?) Another incredible facet of the record-setting run was the sound—because the dragster is electric, its motor was incredibly quiet as it shot down the runway. Maybe they can use it to quickly return books to the shelves in libraries? Shh!

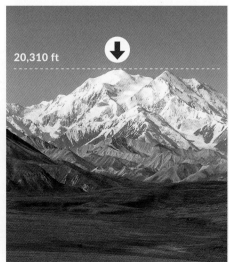

20,310 ft

C. Henry Ford's Quadricycle Conundrum

For a guy who would one day be known as the "genius of the automotive industry," you'd think he'd be better with a tape measure. To get his invention out the door, he had to chop a wider hole in the garage with an ax!

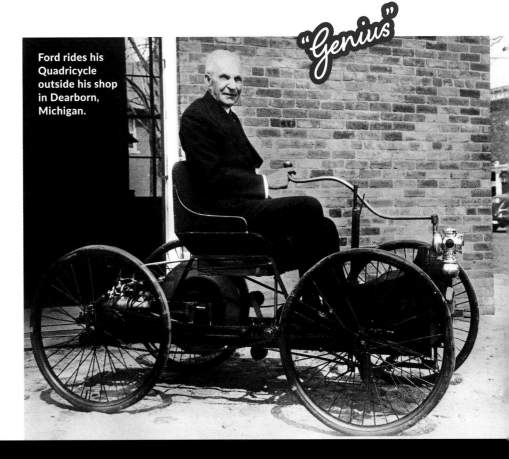

Ford rides his Quadricycle outside his shop in Dearborn, Michigan.

"Genius"

WHAT IS AN URBAN LEGEND?
An urban legend is a made-up story (usually funny or scary) that has details that make it seem like it could be true. Urban legends get told over and over again so many times that people eventually forget they are fake.

Jeep Wrangler JL, Rubicon Trail, 2018

C. A vehicle whose engine delivers power to all four wheels at once

Most vehicles you see on the road either have two-wheel drive (4x2) or four-wheel drive (4x4). Your best bet for not getting stuck while driving off-road over rocks, mud, and snow is a 4x4 because all of the wheels receive power. So if one or two wheels go up in the air, the others are able to keep pushing forward. (P.S. If you guessed a type of wood, we'll give you half credit. Yes, there are wood pieces that measure 4x4, but c'mon, this is a book about motorized vehicles!)

QUESTION 12

Can you identify the construction truck by its shadow?

A. Bulldozer

C. Dump truck

B. Excavator

D. Cement-mixer truck

QUESTION 13

Hot rods are crazy-cool customized race cars that became popular in the 1930s. What's one thing you typically won't find on a vintage hot rod?

A.
Flame paint job

B.
Big rear tires

C.
Windshield wipers

BIGFOOT IS THE NAME OF THE FIRST MONSTER TRUCK—AND OF A LEGENDARY MONSTER-MONSTER! WHICH OF THESE BIGFOOT "FACTS" IS TOTALLY MADE UP?

A.
Bigfoot is also known as Sasquatch.

B.
Bigfoots are said to be seven to nine feet tall.

C.
Bigfoots hate getting haircuts but will sit still if you give them a lollipop.

A

B

C

Turn the page for the answer. >

QUESTION 15

Which of these is a semi truck?

QUESTION 16

What is a chopper?

A. Something that makes dicing onions easier

B. A style of motorcycle with stretched-out handlebars and front forks

C. A motorcycle engine part that "chops" up the gas and air to make it run faster

ANSWER 12

1A, 2D, 3B, 4C

The largest excavator on earth is called the Komatsu D575A-3SD. One scoop of its massive blade can grab 24 tons of dirt and gravel— or even 12 two-ton giraffes!

1932 Ford Roadster

ANSWER 13

C. Windshield wipers

When car nuts first started "hot-rodding," their goal was to make their boring Model T and Model A Fords cooler and lighter. So they hacked the cars up and removed anything they felt was unimportant for speed so the cars could be as light as possible while racing them. That meant removing things like bumpers, hoods, and sometimes even windshields! Faster? Yes. Safer? Um, big no!

ANSWER 14

Bigfoot flies over cars during a California rally in 1989.

C. Bigfoots hate getting haircuts but will sit still if you give them a lollipop.

Okay fine, we actually don't know if that is true or not. If you see Bigfoot, please ask him for us.

BIG FACTS ABOUT BIGFOOT (THE TRUCK)

Bob Chandler created Bigfoot in 1975.

Bigfoot's tires are 10 feet tall.

Bigfoot once jumped a 727 airliner.

There have been 21 versions of Bigfoot over the years, but no Bigfoot 13 because the team says that's an unlucky number.

Bigfoot 16 once held the record for fastest monster truck, speeding along at 86.56 mph!

ANSWER 15

B.

If you guessed A, you were so close! That's a full truck. A "semi" is the part with the engine. And the picture in choice C? We have no idea what that thing is!

ANSWER 16

B. A style of motorcycle with stretched-out handlebars and front forks

Choppers became popular in the 1960s and 1970s. They call them "choppers" because motorcycle enthusiasts who built them would modify (or "chop") factory-built rides and create their own amazing designs, adding elongated forks, wild handlebars, and all kinds of other cool customizations.

QUESTION 17

What in the world is that?

A.
An airplane that forgot to bring its wings to work

B.
A propeller-propelled car

C.
A portable fan for summertime picnics

QUESTION 18

Crash course! What's the name of a very odd sporting event where cars purposely smash into each other until only one is still able to drive?

A. Demolition derby

B. Crash Prix

C. Parking at the mall during the holidays

WHAT IS THE NAME OF THE STYLE OF CARS IN THESE PHOTOS?

A. Mean machines

B. Muscle cars

C. Ridiculous rides

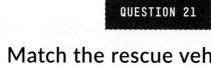

Match the rescue vehicle to the emergency situation:

A

B

C

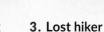

D

1. Blizzard   **2.** Flooding   **3.** Lost hiker   **4.** Fire

Which food mobile would win a drag race?

A. Oscar Mayer Wienermobile

B. Red Bull Mini Cooper

C. World's fastest ice-cream truck

The Bagger 288 is considered the largest land vehicle in the world. The 45,500-ton bucket-wheel excavator is used for mining and is taller than which human-made wonder:

A. The Statue of Liberty

B. George Washington's head on Mount Rushmore

C. Towers of the Brooklyn Bridge

D. All of the above

B. A propeller-propelled car

The 1932 Helicron is a car! Instead of the engine spinning its wheels to make the car move, it spins the propeller, pulling the car forward . . . and terrifying whoever is stopped in front of you at stoplights!

B.
Muscle cars

This was a hard question, as all of the answers do a pretty good job of describing this type of car. Muscle cars became popular in the 1960s and '70s and are known for having big, powerful engines squeezed into boxy two-door coupes. Unlike a sports car that wants to be as aerodynamic and sleek as possible, a muscle car wants to be seen and heard as it rips down the road.

A. Demolition derby

There isn't a clear answer on when and where the first demolition derby occurred, but everyone agrees that these competitions are nuts. Most of the time, you'll see sedans battling it out, but some derbies have featured farm equipment, motorhomes, and even school buses! (And yes, as crazy as it sounds, you do need a driver's license to participate.)

The Shenandoah County Fair's demolition derby in Virginia, August 2012

B. Red Bull Mini Cooper

This battle of drool-inducing rides would be closer than you think. Red Bull's Mini would surely win, with a top speed of 114 mph, but not too far behind would be the frank on wheels. In 1988, race car driver Al Unser Jr. ran some laps in the Wienermobile at Indianapolis Motor Speedway and got it up to 110 mph. That's one hot dog! Coming in last would be the ice-cream truck. In 2020, British car enthusiast Edd China set a Guinness world record for the fastest ride in an electric ice-cream truck, which hit 74 mph. Imagine trying to chase that down the street for a cold treat?

SNO-CAT
Tracks allow it to safely traverse deep snow and slippery ice.

SKEETER HIGH-WATER
Equipped to rescue and carry up to 10 adults from flooded areas.

POLARIS
Small-but-mighty vehicles that can navigate through narrow paths and tough terrain.

WILDLAND FIRE TRUCK
Designed to drive off-road so it can bring water and fire-suppressing foam to wilderness fires.

ANSWER 21

1C, 2A, 3D, 4B

Even more amazing than these rescue vehicles? The brave people who drive them into danger to help those in need.

THE STATUE OF LIBERTY 305 FEET, INCLUDING HER PEDESTAL

GEORGE WASHINGTON'S HEAD ON MOUNT RUSHMORE 60 FEET

ANSWER 22

D. All of the above

Standing 311 feet tall and measuring 705 feet long, this beast gets a lot of work done—it is capable of digging a 98-foot-deep hole the size of a soccer field in a single day!

THE BROOKLYN BRIDGE 272 FEET

Fuhgettaboutit!

QUESTION 23

VS.

Rivian R1T

GMC Hummer EV SUT

WHO WOULD WIN IN A RACE?

Which of these two powerful electric trucks would win in a tug of war?

QUESTION 24

What in the world is this?

A. Toyota's innovative crash-test dummy

B. A Toyota-built robot that is really good at basketball

C. A very, very high-tech toaster oven

The Falcon 8x8 is a fire truck built to handle airport emergencies. It's the largest fire truck in the world. How much water do you think it can hold?

A.
Enough to fill 4755 one-gallon milk containers

B.
Three Olympic-size swimming pools

C.
The Atlantic Ocean

What in the world is this?

A. A very strange parking lot

B. The end result of the first demolition derby

C. Carhenge, an art installation that mimics the mystical Stonehenge

Can you guess the name of the first tank ever made for military combat?

A. Boom-Boom Barry

B. Large Larry

C. Little Willie

VS.

WHICH WOULD WIN IN A RACE?

A hypercar or a tsunami?

Seriously Silly Question

In the spoof version of the song "Jingle Bells," what happened when the Batmobile lost its wheel?

A. Robin changed the tire.

B. Batman finished his journey on the Bat-tricycle.

C. The Joker got away.

Rivian R1T

Trucks are tested for, among other things, their towing capacity (a.k.a. how much they can haul via a trailer). The stronger truck in this contest—we actually tested them head to head in 2022!—is the quad-motor Rivian R1T, able to tow 11,000 pounds compared to the three-motor Hummer's 7500-pound max. Better hit the gym, Hummer!

A. Enough to fill 4755 one-gallon milk containers

Most fire trucks can hold about 1500 gallons of water—this one can hold 4755. With that much water, the massive machine can race down airport runways to extinguish airplane fire emergencies (or quench a lot of people's thirst).

B. A Toyota-built robot that is really good at basketball

While many car companies use robotic machines to build cars on the assembly line, Toyota has been busy for years building human-like robots that can do way more than attach a fender to a frame. In 2022, this one, named CUE6, rolled out during halftime of an Alvark Tokyo vs. Shiga Lakes game in Japan and wowed the crowd by draining shot after shot. Get this guy an NBA contract!

HERO JEEP
In 1942, a Jeep used by American soldiers was hit during a Japanese attack and got two holes in its windshield but still managed to function. Nicknamed "Old Faithful," the Jeep received the Purple Heart, an award usually given to military personnel wounded in combat, from its impressed occupants. After taking those hits, it continued carrying out its job of transporting high-ranking personnel for another year before it was retired.

C. Little Willie

Built in 1915 to give British soldiers an advantage in the trench warfare of World War I, Little Willie weighed 16 tons and chugged along at 3.5 mph.

The real Stonehenge in England

ANSWER 27

C. Carhenge

In 1987, artist Jim Reinders created a stunning (and let's face it, weird) replica of England's Stonehenge in Nebraska. He made it out of 38 vintage cars, all spray-painted gray to resemble Stonehenge's massive and mysterious stones.

ANSWER 28 | Tsunami

Most hypercars can easily top 200 mph. That sounds fast, but it's not as fast as tsunami waves, which can race across the ocean at over 500 mph before surfacing at the shore as a devastating wall of water.

DANGER TSUNAMI

ANSWER 29 **C. THE JOKER GOT AWAY.**

Sing it loud!

Jingle bells,
Batman smells,
Robin laid an egg.
The Batmobile
lost its wheel,
and the Joker got away—hey!

CHAPTER SIX

ROAD WARRIOR

Don't get lost

on this amazing

trivia trip.

Turn the page for the answer. >

QUESTION 1

What does SUV stand for?

A. Super-ugly vehicle
B. Sport-utility vehicle
C. Sorta-useful vehicle

S

B. Sport-utility vehicle

SUVs come in three sizes: compact, mid-size, and full-size. But no matter how big, they all have one thing in common—they're built to get things done, whether that is cruising over rough terrain or hauling giant packages of toilet paper home from Costco.

Vanity license plates are personalized plates that car owners pay a little extra money to have. In 2023, someone paid a lot extra to secure the plate "P 7" in Dubai. How much do you think they paid for it at auction?

A. $150

B. $15,000

C. $15 million

A stretch of road near Challa, Bolivia, in 2012

QUESTION 3

THE MOST dangerous street in the world is called: **A.** Ouch Avenue **B.** Death Road **C.** Accident Alley

QUESTION 4

Who makes the most? Put these car-manufacturing countries in order of the most to the least autos built there.

A. China
B. United States
C. Japan
D. Tatooine

QUESTION 5

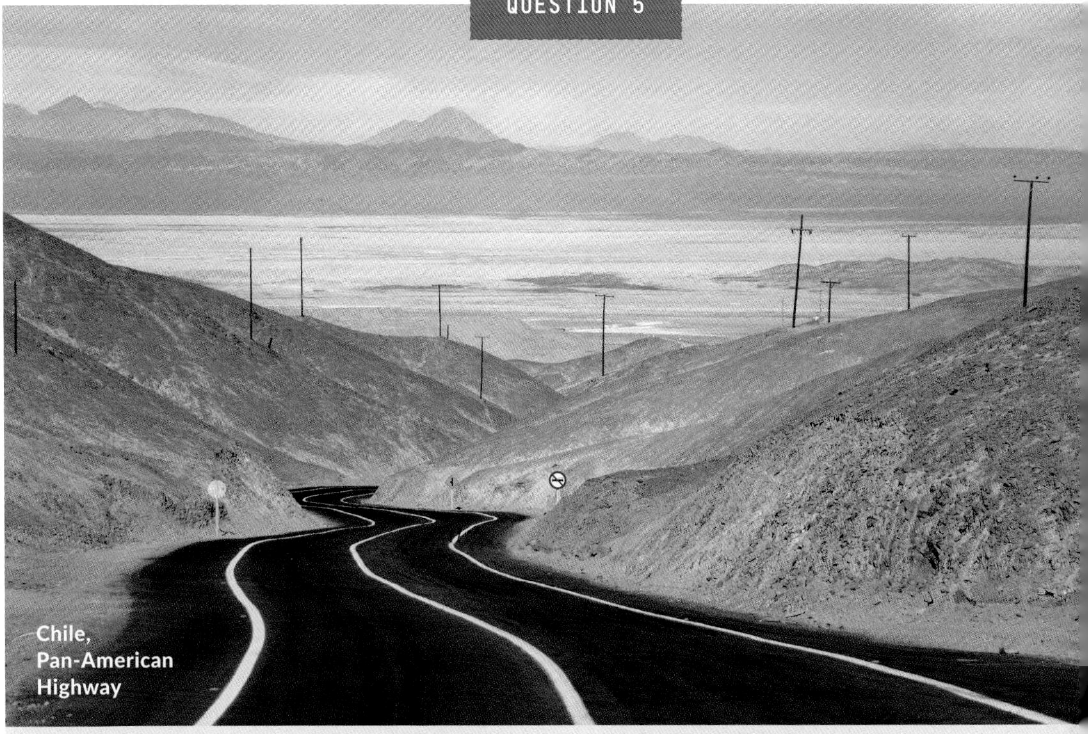

Chile, Pan-American Highway

The Pan-American Highway is the longest motorway in the world. If you drove its entire 19,000-mile length, which of these things would you see?

A. A volcano
B. Jungles
C. Glaciers
D. All of the above

QUESTION 6

LOGO LINEUP

Match the emblem with the car-maker.

AUDI MAZDA TESLA HYUNDAI INFINITI

C. $15 million

In an auction that raised money for the food charity 1 Billion Meals Endowment, an anonymous bidder beat the competition with a staggering $15 million bid. That's $7.5 million per character! P 7 earned a lot of dough for that food charity, as well as a spot in history as the most expensive license plate ever (so far, anyway!). Dubai's ultra-wealthy residents have a history of spending tons of money on vanity plates for fundraising efforts. A different buyer spent almost $9 million for D 5, explaining that his favorite number is nine, and if you add "D" (the fourth letter of the alphabet) with five, you get nine. It might seem a little crazy, but when it comes to prestigious low-number UAE (United Arab Emirates) license plates, it seems anything goes!

DID YOU KNOW?
There are nearly 1.5 billion cars on the road throughout the world right now!

Beep beep!

ANSWER 4

A, C, B, D

The latest stats reveal that China is by far the biggest carmaking country in the world, pumping out 26.08 million vehicles in 2021. That makes sense, since China has a population of 1.4 billion—that's a lot of people who need a ride! The U.S. created 9.17 million, Japan 7.85 million, and Tatooine? Well, it's a planet, not a country, and Luke Skywalker's X-34 Landspeeder didn't have any wheels, so we're going to give them a zero.

ANSWER 3

B. Death Road

The North Yungas Road in Bolivia is nicknamed "Death Road" because the narrow mountain road features blinding fog, 15,000-foot drops, and no guardrails in many sections. Hundreds of travelers each year never make it to their destination.

D. All of the above

The Pan-American Highway stretches from the southernmost tip of South America all the way up to the Arctic Ocean in Alaska. It weaves its way through 14 countries and over a mountain in Costa Rica called the Summit of Death. It gets extremely cold up there and before there was a road, many people died trying to cross it on foot or horseback. Thinking about driving the entire length of the Pan-American Highway? Load up a whole lot of songs on your driving playlist. If you drive eight hours a day, it would take you about three months to make the full trip.

There is more than meets the eye at first glance of these logos.

AUDI	HYUNDAI	MAZDA	TESLA	INFINITI
The four circles represent the four German car companies that joined together to form the one.	The "H" is designed to look like two people shaking hands.	The "M" has a pair of wings representing the company's desire to soar to new heights.	Its "T" looks like the cross section of an electric motor.	Its logo looks like a road heading off into the horizon.

QUESTION 7

During the making of the flicks in this automobile movie franchise, an estimated 2000 cars have been wrecked. One poor car was dropped from an airplane, and the parachute didn't open. Ouch! What is the name of the movie franchise?

A. *Cars*

B. *The Fast and the Furious*

C. *Willy Wonka and the Chocolate Car Factory*

Every year, millions of people visit Yellowstone National Park in their cars. If a bear approaches your car, what do the park rangers recommend you do?

A.
Honk your horn.

B.
Roll down your window and offer it a snack.

C.
Get out and cozy up for the coolest selfie ever!

QUESTION 8

You may have noticed that there are three different fuel choices at the gas pump. Each choice has a different number, called its octane rating. Octanes usually range from 87 to 94. What does a higher octane of gas do?

A. Makes cars go slower

B. Reduces knocking in the engine

C. Tastes better on pancakes

QUESTION 10

On average, how long
do traffic lights stay red?

A. Two minutes
B. 60–90 seconds
C. 15 hours

QUESTION 11

Back in 2000, several drivers on
Interstate 95 near the border of
Virginia and North Carolina
alerted police that someone was
throwing bananas and crab apples
at passing cars. Why weren't the
offenders arrested?

A. The throwers got away.
B. The fruit came flying from a
supermarket that exploded.
C. The fruit-flingers were monkeys.

QUESTION 12

What is the name of a style of car
that has a retractable roof?

A. Convertible   B. Bad-Hair-Day Delight   C. Wind Whipper

123

B. *The Fast and the Furious*

The car-crashing franchise has destroyed a lot of amazing rides, but the series has made billions of dollars, so the producers can afford the repair bills!

B. Reduces knocking in the engine

Knock, knock. Who's there? Cheap gas in your engine! Have you ever heard a knocking and rumbling noise from a running engine? That's not the engine parts rattling around—the noise is caused by fuel burning unevenly in the cylinders. Higher-octane gas is designed to burn more evenly, which more positively affects an engine's lifespan and performance. That's why fancy cars only drink the fanciest of gasoline. Cheers!

A. Honk your horn.

A 700-or-so-pound Grizzly bear with razor-sharp claws is not a teddy bear, so no feeding or cuddling! Honking will likely spook the wild animal and send it running for cover (where it will probably get made fun of by its buddy bears for being such a scaredy-cat).

ANSWER 10

B. 60–90 seconds

SOMEHOW IT ALWAYS FEELS LIKE 15 HOURS!

WAIT TIME

Using 75 seconds as the average, and taking into account driving stats from AAA, Yahoo estimates that the average person who commutes to work in a car will spend 4.7 months of their life sitting at red lights. Hope you have some good tunes with you!

ANSWER 11

C. The fruit-flingers were monkeys.

Police believe that the pesky primates throwing the fruit had escaped from their handlers on the way to an appearance at a nearby fair. Talk about monkey business!

ANSWER 12

A. Convertible

1927 Austin 7 Chummy

At first, cars didn't have roofs and people wanted roofs. So then carmakers put roofs on cars and people missed having the wind in their hair. In 1927, Buick, Cadillac, Lincoln, and Chrysler were among the manufacturers offering convertibles with roofs that could roll up or down. Happy now, people?

Americans like their roadside attractions weird—and the bigger the better! Can you put these oversize oddities in order from biggest to smallest?

A.
WORLD'S TALLEST THERMOMETER
Baker, California

B.
WORLD'S LARGEST FISH STATUE
Hayward, Wisconsin

C.
WORLD'S LARGEST BALL OF TWINE
Cawker City, Kansas

World's Largest
Ball of Sisal Twine
Started by Frank Stoeber in 1953
8,083,640 FEET   20,078 POUNDS

D.
WORLD'S LARGEST KETCHUP BOTTLE
Collinsville, Illinois

WHAT ARE MOST ROADS MADE OF ANYWAY?

A. Asphalt

B. Old fudge

C. A very rare element called streetonium

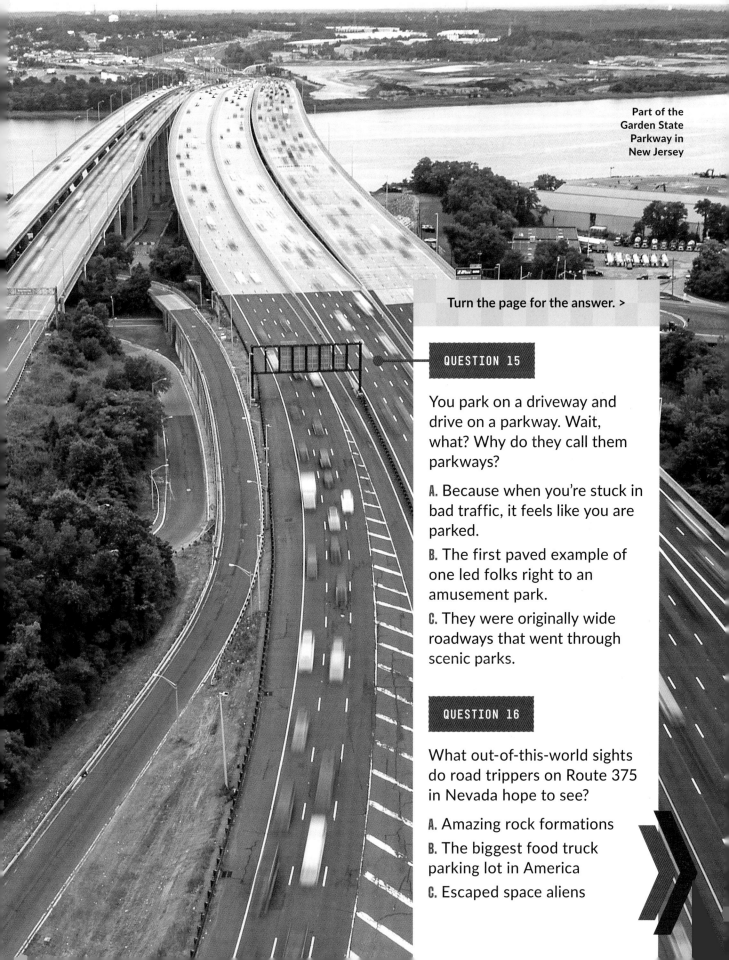

Part of the
Garden State
Parkway in
New Jersey

Turn the page for the answer. >

QUESTION 15

You park on a driveway and drive on a parkway. Wait, what? Why do they call them parkways?

A. Because when you're stuck in bad traffic, it feels like you are parked.

B. The first paved example of one led folks right to an amusement park.

C. They were originally wide roadways that went through scenic parks.

QUESTION 16

What out-of-this-world sights do road trippers on Route 375 in Nevada hope to see?

A. Amazing rock formations

B. The biggest food truck parking lot in America

C. Escaped space aliens

D. 170 FEET TALL, INCLUDING ITS TOWER

B. 41 FEET TALL, 143 FEET LONG

A. 134 FEET TALL

C. 40 FEET TALL AND WIDE

If you're wondering why anyone thought it'd be exciting to make the world's biggest ball of twine, keep wondering because we sure don't know!

ANSWER 14

A. Asphalt

Asphalt is a mix of gravel, sand, and a goopy byproduct from crude-oil refining. The National Asphalt Pavement Association estimates that 2.6 million miles of road in America are paved with asphalt—enough to circle the world almost 100 times!

SLIP 'N SLIDE
The McMurdo–South Pole Highway in Antarctica is actually paved with snow! Only special vehicles with snow treads drive on it—very carefully.

The Blue Ridge Parkway in North Carolina

ANSWER 15

C. They were originally wide roadways that went through scenic parks.

The first modern parkway in America was the Bronx River Parkway, which opened in 1925. At the time, it was designed for cars and horse-drawn buggies to share the road. These days only cars are allowed to drive on it. Sorry, horsies!

C. Escaped space aliens

Nicknamed the "Extraterrestrial Highway," Route 375 passes by Area 51, the top-secret U.S. military base where some believe government scientists house aliens. "E.T. phone Uber?"

Before blinkers—the signal lights that indicate which way a car is turning—how did drivers alert others on the road when they were about to turn?

A. Used hand signals

B. Shouted "Left!" or "Right!" out the window

C. Held arrow signs out the window

WHAT IS A DRIVETRAIN?

A. Special train that transports cars from the factory to the dealership

B. All of a car's components that create power and transmit it to the wheels

C. Vehicle that makes fun *choo-choo* noises when you drive over 50 mph

What is the name of the famous road that stretches—albeit interrupted now—from Chicago to Los Angeles and in its heyday was known as the "Main Street of America"?

A. Route 66

B. I-95

C. I-Don't Know

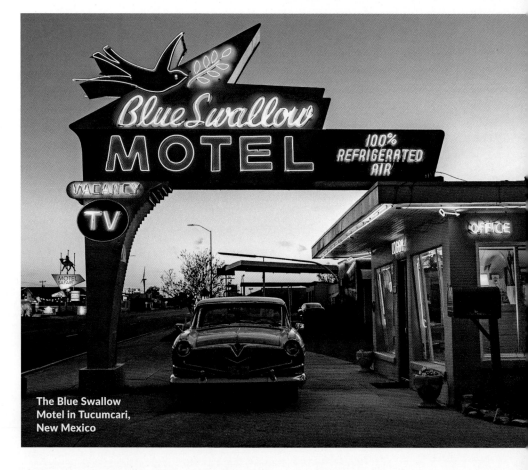

The Blue Swallow Motel in Tucumcari, New Mexico

Buggin' Out: All of these insect-inspired auto names are real—except one. Can you swat the fake?

A
Hudson
Hornet

B
Dodge Charger
Super Bee

C
Alfa Romeo
Spider

D
Honda
Flea

The Audtobahn
A3 motorway
connecting
Würzburg and
Frankfurt
in Germany

The autobahn is a famous highway system in Germany.
What is so special about it?

A. It has the most chocolate-shop rest stops in the world.

B. You're allowed to drive as fast as you want in some sections.

C. You're only allowed to drive BMWs and Volkswagens on it.

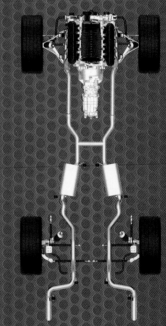

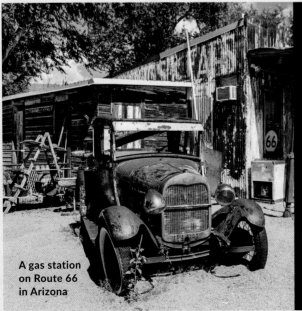

A. Used hand signals

An arm held straight out meant they were making a left, an arm bent at the elbow and pointing up meant going right, and pointing down meant stopping. Two fingers up? That means "Peace out."

B. All of a car's components that create power and transmit it to the wheels

A. Route 66

(If you got it wrong, then technically C is also a correct answer.) Route 66 is no longer a fully functioning highway, but much of the original route is still drivable with careful planning, and sections of it have been preserved as historical spots you can still visit.

THE SECRET DIRECTIONS IN ROUTE NUMBERS
Routes with odd numbers run north and south, and even-numbered ones go east and west.

A gas station on Route 66 in Arizona

The drivetrain is a collection of parts—including but not limited to the transmission, differential, driveshaft, and axles—working together to make a car to move. We love teamwork!

D. Honda Flea

Sure fleas can hop around pretty fast, but we can't imagine it'd be very comfortable squishing into a vehicle named after a tiny bug that makes people itchy.

HUDSON HORNET

DODGE CHARGER SUPER BEE

Autobahn

B. You're allowed to drive as fast as you want in some sections.

Most sections of the autobahn system have signs recommending a speed limit of 130 km/h (81 mph), but there are others where the only limit is your car's engine (and your tolerance for scary-high speeds!).

ALFA ROMEO SPIDER

WHAT DO THESE ROAD SIGNS MEAN?

A. _____

B. _____

C. _____

D. _____

E. _____

QUESTION 22

Can you match the nickname to the ride?

1. Punch Buggy
2. Woody
3. Bimmer
4. Tin Lizzie

A. BMW M3 CS

B. AMC Eagle

C. Ford Model T

D. Volkswagen Beetle

QUESTION 24

DETROIT is the center of America's carmaking universe. What is its nickname?
A. Tire Town   **B.** Motor City   **C.** Vroom Village

QUESTION 25

What does HOV stand for in HOV lane?

A. High-occupancy vehicle
B. High-octane vehicle
C. High-odor vehicle

QUESTION 26

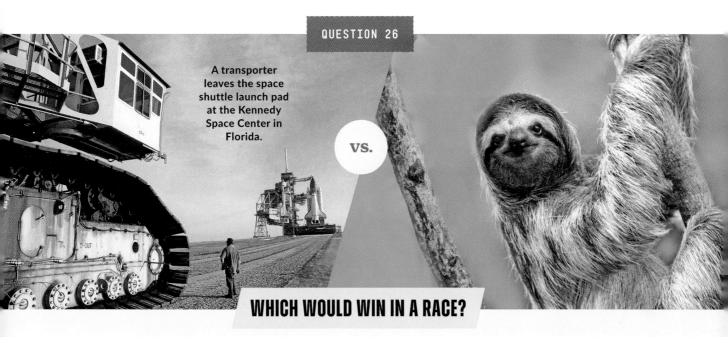

A transporter leaves the space shuttle launch pad at the Kennedy Space Center in Florida.

VS.

WHICH WOULD WIN IN A RACE?

Space-shuttle launch pad vs. three-toed sloth

Seriously Silly Question

QUESTION 27

Which of these street names is fake?

A. Butts Station Road
B. Booger Branch Road
C. No Name Lane
D. They're all real

1D, 2B, 3A, 4C

BMW'S nickname started off as "Beemer," which was used to differentiate its motorcycles from a competitor whose bikes were known as Beezers. Eventually, BMW enthusiasts adopted "Bimmer" for their cars.

WOODIES like the AMC Eagle pictured here were a super-popular style of station wagon. At one point, they were made with actual wood paneling, but after the 1950s, the switch was made to fake wood. Good news for people worried about splinters, bad news for hungry termites.

THE MODEL T'S nickname origin is thought to be that a famous Model T race car was named "Old Liz."

PUNCH BUGGY is a name whose origin is unknown, but everyone knows that the game—where you punch someone in the arm if you see a VW Beetle—hurts!

A. Hospital

B. No U-Turn

C. Hill Ahead

D. Slippery When Wet

E. School Crossing

Study these signs and more—when you are old enough to go for your driver's permit, they're gonna be on the test, trust us!

Experts test engines in a plant in Detroit, Michigan, in 1915.

B. Motor City

Detroit, Michigan—better known as "Motor City" or "Motown" (a combination of "motor" and "town")—became the capital of car manufacturing in America in the early 1900s in part because of its prime location. The raw materials needed to build cars were all easy to bring in via the Great Lakes waterways and railroads, and the finished cars were similarly easy to ship out. (It also didn't hurt that Henry Ford, one of the most successful auto innovators in history, lived there.)

A. High-occupancy vehicle

During busy traffic times, the HOV lane is open only to vehicles with two or more people inside. The idea is to encourage ridesharing, which reduces the number of cars on the road (and so reduces traffic) and benefits the environment too.

ANSWER 26

SPACE-SHUTTLE LAUNCH PAD

The launch pad would win in the world's most boring race. Sloths crawl along at 0.15 mph, while the massive mobile launch pad moves at around 2 mph. We doubt the sloth would be upset to lose—or that it would even show up to the race. They sometimes sleep 20 hours a day!

ANSWER 27

D. They're all real

There is a Butts Station Road in Virginia, a Booger Branch Road in Georgia, and a No Name Lane in Florida. Who wants to go on a really weird road trip to all three?

CAR-PEDIA

A glossary of car

terms on the go!

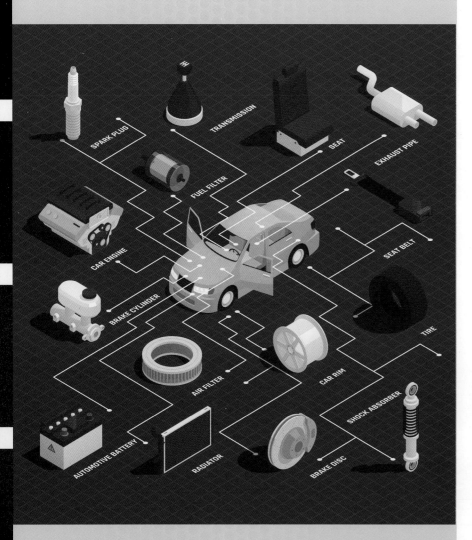

SPARK PLUG · TRANSMISSION · SEAT · EXHAUST PIPE · FUEL FILTER · CAR ENGINE · SEAT BELT · BRAKE CYLINDER · AIR FILTER · CAR RIM · TIRE · AUTOMOTIVE BATTERY · RADIATOR · SHOCK ABSORBER · BRAKE DISC

ABS (Anti-Lock Braking System): Senses when any of the car's wheels have locked up—or are about to—and automatically reduces the braking forces to keep them rolling and prevent dangerous skids.

Aerodynamics: How air flows around a car's body.

Airbags: Air-filled cushions that instantaneously pop out during an accident to protect people in a vehicle.

Air filter: Catches dirt and other particles from the air in an engine.

Alternator: Powers the electrical system in cars (headlights, air conditioners, entertainment system, etc.).

Axle: The bars that connect tires together. In most vehicles, there is a front axle that connects the two front wheels and a rear axle that connects the rear wheels.

Battery: Provides the electricity used to start a car.

Body: A vehicle's shape and design.

Brakes: The system that slows down and stops a car.

Bumper: A band made of metal or plastic that reduces the amount of damage done to the car's body if it hits something or vice versa.

Chassis: The base frame of a vehicle to which all of its parts are attached.

Combustion engine: An engine that gets its power from burning fuel and oxygen.

Convertible: A vehicle with a roof that can either roll down or be removed.

Coupe: A fixed-roof, usually two-door passenger car.

Crankshaft: A bar that transforms the up-and-down motion of an engine's pistons into spinning motion for the vehicle's tires.

Cylinder: The part of the engine that contains the pistons. They mostly come in pairs. Most of the cars you see on the road have four or six cylinders.

Downforce: A force created by airflow that pushes a car body down to the road.

Drive range: How far a vehicle can go before it needs to be recharged or before its engine requires more gasoline.

Drivetrain: All of the car parts (besides the engine) that work together to bring power to the wheels.

Emissions: Gasses given off by a car due to burning fuel.

EV: Electric vehicle

Fiberglass: A light material used for car bodies that is made of small glass fibers.

Force: Something that causes an object to move, slow down, or stop.

Fuel injection: The system that sends fuel into the engine.

Fuel economy: How far a vehicle can travel using the gas in its tank, usually measured in mpg (miles per gallon).

Handling: Describes how well a car is able to steer in various driving situations.

Headlights: Bright white lights in the front of the car that allow drivers to see in the dark.

Horsepower: The unit of measure of an engine's power.

Hot rod: A car (usually an old one) that has been modified to go faster and look radder.

Hypercars: The most extreme cars ever made when it comes to speed, performance, tech innovation, and looking like something a supervillain would drive.

Gear: A circular machine part that determines how much power and speed is given by an engine. A lower gear delivers more power for doing things like climbing a steep hill. A higher gear delivers more flat-out speed.

GPS (Global Positioning System): A navigation device that uses information from satellites to find your current location and uses digital maps to tell you the best way to get to a destination.

Mirrors: Rearview and side-view mirrors help drivers see if anything is behind them when they are backing up or changing lanes. (And the mirror in the visor helps you see if you have anything gross in your nose before you get out.)

MPH (miles per hour): The standard unit of measure of a vehicle's speed primarily used in America and the U.K.

Muffler: Part of the exhaust system that makes a car quieter. Shh!

Oil: Reduces wear and tear on an engine's moving parts and prevents overheating.

Power: The rate at which work is performed.

Power steering: A system that makes it easier for a driver to turn the steering wheel of a car.

Powertrain: A term for an engine and its transmission.

Production cars: Identical models of cars that are made in large quantities and sold to the public (e.g., Toyota Corolla or Chevy Camaro).

Prototype: The first model of a car that is tested and developed.

Radiator: A vital part of the engine that uses coolant fluid, a fan, and hoses to help stop a car's engine from getting too hot.

Redline: The maximum recommended rpm of an engine before it will get damaged.

RPM (revolutions per minute): The unit of measure for how fast the crankshaft rotates all the way around, which translates to how fast the car moves.

Sedan: A fixed-roof car that usually has four doors and always has a roomy back-seat area.

Spoiler: A device fixed to the back of a car that creates more downforce, which increases the tires' grip on the road.

Street-legal: All the things (like seatbelts, headlights, and working brakes) that allow a vehicle to be safely operated on public roads.

Supercar: A special type of car that is street-legal, extremely fast, looks incredibly cool, and because of all of those things is ridiculously expensive.

Supercharger: An air compressor that forces more air into an engine to produce more power.

Suspension: A system that helps protect your car and can make a ride more comfortable over rough terrain or uneven roads.

Taillights: Red lights on the back of a car that help it be seen at night.

Tire pressure: How much air is in a vehicle's tires, measured in psi (pounds per square inch).

Torque: A twisting force produced by the crankshaft.

Trim level: The level of fanciness of a car's look and abilities, like leather seats inside and big cool tires outside or more horsepower and safety features.

Turbine: A device that uses gases to spin and create energy.

Turbocharger: A kind of supercharger that produces more power for a car by using exhaust gasses to spin a turbine.

VIN (vehicle identification number): A car's identifying code. Every vehicle on the road has its own number.

INDEX

INDEX

CREDITS

Cover: Courtesy of Lamborghini; Getty Images
Inside and Back Cover: Adobe Stock

Getty Images 1, 3, 6, 7, 10, 13, 14, 16, 18, 21, 22, 24, 38, 41, 44, 46, 47, 51, 55, 58, 62, 63, 65, 69, 77, 93, 98, 102, 104, 105, 107, 109, 110, 111, 112, 113, 115, 119, 120, 121, 122, 123, 125, 127, 128, 131, 132, 134, 135, 137, 144 Adobe Stock 2, 6, 7, 10, 12, 14, 16, 17, 18, 23, 25, 32, 39, 41, 46, 50, 54, 64, 65, 96, 105, 115, 123, 124, 126, 132, 133, 134, 137, 138 Genesis 4–5 General Motors 6 (motor), 28 (Corvette), 29, 31, 58 (logo), 100, 102 (truck), 112 (GMC) Jaguar 7, 15 Ferrari 9, 30, 45, 85 (steering wheel) Stellantis 11, 43 (Citroen), 44 (Citroen), 103 (Jeep), 108 (Dodge) Mack 11 (Mack) Rolls Royce 11 (Rolls Royce), 40, 42, 43 Michel Porro/Getty Images 11 (dancing elephant) Wolfgang/Adobe Stock 11 (Bugatti) Dreamworks Motorsports 13 (hood ornament) Paul Chinn/The San Francisco Chronicle via Getty Images 18 (mule car) BMW 19, 134 Lamborghini 19, 26–27, 28, 32, 36, 42, 44, 46 Toyota 19 Drako Motors 19 MIGUEL MEDINA/AFP via Getty Images 20 Chris Crisman Photography 22 (Eta), 24 PAU BARRENA/AFP via Getty Images 22 (robot) Harley Davidson 22 (motorcycle) Tommaso Boddi/WireImage 22 (Polaris) Honda 22 (ATV), 28, 30, 51 (bike), 59 Marc Witt-Fantasy Junction 25 (amphibious car) Brandon Woyshnis/Adobe Stock 28 (Ferrari) Bugatti 28, 45 McLaren 28, 32, 36 Porche 28, 39 Ford 28, 98 (truck), 108 (Mustang) Aston Martin 32, 35 VanderWolf Images/Adobe Stock 32 Filip Gränström/Koenigsegg 32 Benedict Redgrove 32 Bernard Cahier/Getty Images 32 edvvc www.flickr.com 32 Pagani 32 Rimac 33, 35 Goddard Archive 2/Alamy Stock Photo 35 Entertainment Pictures/Alamy Stock Photo 36 liubomir118809/Adobe Stock 36 Courtesy of Bugatti and Lego 36, 38 Keizo Mori/UPI/Shutterstock 36 Khayat Nicolas/ABACA/Shutterstock 37 Gabe Ginsberg/Getty Images 37 Kris Connor/Getty Images 37 PictureLux/The Hollywood Archive/Alamy Stock Photo 37 Barrett-Jackson via Getty Images 38 Patrick SICCOLI/Gamma-Rapho via Getty Images 38 rosinka79/Adobe Stock 38 Dreamworks/Kobal/Shutterstock 39 Ali Haider/EPA/Shutterstock 39 ArtEvent ET 40 Vladimir Zhoga/Shutterstock 42 Hennessey 43 Nissan 43 Mercedes Benz Public Archive 43 Tom Pennington/Getty Images 44 (Phelps) Amy Sussman/Getty Images 45 (Lady Gaga) Mason Poole/Parkwood Media/Getty Images for Atlantis The Royal 45 (Beyonce) ANGELA WEISS/AFP via Getty Images 45 (The Rock) Roy Rochlin/Getty Images 45 (Hart) David M. Benett/Dave Benett/WireImage 45 (Cena) Sergey Kohl/Adobe Stock 45 (Chevy) Drive Images / Alamy Stock Photo 45 (Rolls) Courtesy Salvaggiodesign.com 45 (Plymouth) ©CITROEN COMMUNICATION 46 (Sahara)

Daily Herald Archive/National Science & Media Museum/SSPL via Getty Images 48–49 Culture Club/Getty Images 50 EDU Vision/Alamy Stock Photo 51 Lucille Cottin/Adobe Stock 51 Great Choice - stock.adobe.com 51 Courtesy Audi 52, 119 Bettmann/Contributor 53, 68, 103 Godong/Universal Images Group via Getty Images 53 (logo) ullstein bild/ullstein bild via Getty Images 54, 68 NASA 55 (moon), 67 (Lunar Roving), 69 Ann Cutting/Stockimo/Alamy Stock Photo 56 INTERFOTO/Alamy Stock Photo 56 bilwissedition Ltd. & Co. KG/Alamy Stock Photo 57 John Roe 57 (Saab) Barrett-Jackson via Getty Images 57 (Delorean) Drive Images/Alamy Stock Photo 57 (Saturn) Ardasavasciogullari 57 (Pontiac) OlegMirabo 57 (Oldsmobile) Stefan Lambauer 58 (Beetle) dbvirago/Adobe Stock 58 (Matchbox) Stasiuk/Adobe stock 58 (Hot Wheels) George Rinhart/Corbis via Getty Images 59 FREERS PHOTOGRAPHY LLC/Ford 59 Mercedes 59, 61 Volkswagen US Media Site 60 John Stillwell - PA Images/PA Images via Getty Images 60 (Matchbox) SplashNews.com 60 (Hot Wheels) North Wind Picture Archives/Alamy Stock Photo 61 Solent News/Shutterstock 62 o1559kip/Adobe Stock 62 Universal History Archive/Universal Images Group via Getty Images 65 (McKinley) Media Drum World/Alamy Stock Photo 65 National Motor Museum/Shutterstock 65 V. Pawlowski/ullstein bild via Getty Images 66 National Motor Museum/Heritage Images/Getty Images 67 NASA/JPL-Caltech 67 (Mars Rover) Kypros/Getty Images 71 Monty Fresco/ANL/Shutterstock 72 The Evel Knievel Museum and K and K Promotions, Inc. 72 (Honda) Pat Brollier/The Enthusiast Network via Getty Images/Getty Images 72 (Triumph) Keystone/Hulton Archive/Getty Images 72 (Harley) Michael Ochs Archives/Getty Images 73 David Madison/Getty Images 74 (speed) John Harrelson/Getty Images for NASCAR 74 (Dominos) Jeffrey Vest/Icon Sportswire via Getty Images 74 (Huggies), 76, 87 Sean Gardner/Getty Images 74 (Swiffer) Darrian Traynor/Getty Images for SATC 75 Corrado Millanta/Klemantaski Collection/Getty Images 76 (race) David Madison/Getty Images 76 (ThrustSSC) ISC Archives/CQ-Roll Call Group via Getty Images 77 (Guthrie) Jakub Porzycki/NurPhoto via Getty Images 77 (Ferrari) Chris Graythen/Getty Images 78 ,79 ISC Archives/CQ-Roll Call Group via Getty Images 80 (beach) James Gilbert/Getty Images 80 (milk) Clive Rose/Getty Images 81 Matthew Richardson/Alamy Stock Photo 82 (wheelie) Will Lester/Icon Sportswire via Getty Images 82 (flag) Jamie Squire/Getty Images 82 (vertical lights) Mark Thompson / Allsport 82 (horizontal lights) Ian West/PA Images via Getty Images 83 Sam Morris/Icon

Sportswire via Getty Images 84 Retrieved from the Library of Congress 84 Rudy Carezzevoli/Getty Images 85 Felipe Trueba - PA Images/PA Images via Getty Images 85 Bryn Lennon/Getty Images 86 Pius Koller/imageBROKER/Shutterstock 88 ORSTEN BLACKWOOD/AFP via Getty Images 88 Rusty Jarrett/Getty Images 89 John Harrelson/Getty Images for NASCAR 89 Jeff Gross/Getty Images 90 ISC Archives/CQ-Roll Call Group via Getty Images 90 (Scott) Elsa/Getty Images 90 (Jordan) Jared C. Tilton/Getty Images 90 (Wallace) Tasos Katopodis/Getty Images 90 (Jackson) Steph Chambers/Getty Images 90 (Shohei) Kia 90 Dan Sanger/Icon Sportswire via Getty Images 91 Joe Marino - Bill Cantrell/UPI/Shutterstock 92 Harry How/Getty Images 92 Jeffrey Brown/Icon Sportswire via Getty Images 93 Larry Marano/Shutterstock 95 James Atoa/UPI/Shutterstock 96 Shutterstock 96 (peanut car) Felix Lipov/Shutterstock 96 (popemobile) Lucasfilm/Fox/Kobal/Shutterstock 97 Britta Pedersen-Pool/Getty Images 97 Massimo Valicchia/NurPhoto via Getty Images 98 (popemobile) Noam Galai/Getty Images 98 (Mr. Peanut) RGR Collection/Alamy Stock Photo 99 (Spongebob) Joe Raedle/Getty Images 99 SpaceX/Flickr 99 Magic Car Pics/Shutterstock 101 Universal History Archive/Universal Images Group via Getty Images 101 (Ford) Paul Martinez 106 (hot rod) Tim Defrisco/Getty Images 106 (Bigfoot) Oscar Mayer 109 SVI 109 (fire truck) Alizada Studios/Shutterstock 109 (snocat) Skeeter 109 (flood truck) Polaris 109 (cart) Matt McClain for The Washington Post via Getty Images 110 (derby) jetcityimage/stock.adobe.com 110 Rivian 112, 114 KAZUHIRO NOGI/AFP via Getty Images 112 (robot) ARFF 112 Sueddeutsche Zeitung Photo/Alamy Stock Photo 113 (tank) Education Images/Universal Images Group via Getty Images 113 THOMAS COEX/AFP via Getty Images 114 (robot) AP Photo/U.S. Marine Corps 114 Silver Screen Collection/Getty Images 115 Land Rover 117 AIZAR RALDES/AFP via Getty Images 118 Hyundai 119 Infiniti 119 Mazda 119 Courtesy of Tesla, Inc 119 Moviestore/Shutterstock 124 National Motor Museum/Heritage Images/Getty Images 125 (car) PG/Bauer-Griffin/GC Images 126 (thermometer) Franck Fotos/Alamy Stock Photo 126 (fish) Larry Porges/Shutterstock 126 (bottle) MelissaMN/Adobe Stock 130 OlegMirabo/Adobe Stock 133 (Hornet, Spider) Gestalt Imagery/shutterstock 133 (Dodge) Christopher Ziemnowicz 134 (AMC) ulstein bild via Getty Images 134 (Ford) Luca Piccini Basile/Adobe Stock 134 (VW) Universal History Archive/Universal Images Group via Getty Images 136

Icons throughout: Noun Project

143

Book design by Jennifer Utschig
and Valery Sorokin

Library of Congress Cataloging-in-Publication
Data available on request
10 9 8 7 6 5 4 3 2 1

Published by Hearst Home, an imprint of Hearst
Books/Hearst Communications, Inc.
300 W 57th Street
New York, NY 10019

Car and Driver is a registered trademark of
Hearst Autos, Inc. Hearst Home Kids, the Hearst
Home Kids logo, and Hearst Books are registered
trademarks of Hearst Communications, Inc.

For information about custom editions,
special sales, premium and corporate purchases:
hearst.com/magazines/hearst-books

Printed in China
ISBN 978-1-958395-77-6